D1304463

THE WORLD AT LARGE

THE PUBLICATION OF THIS BOOK WAS SUPPORTED BY A GRANT FROM THE ERIC MATHIEU KING FUND OF THE ACADEMY OF AMERICAN POETS

Phoenix Poets

A SERIES EDITED BY ALAN SHAPIRO

James McMichael

THE WORLD AT LARGE

New and Selected Poems, 1971–1996

THE UNIVERSITY OF CHICAGO PRESS   *Chicago & London*

James McMichael is professor of English and comparative literature at the University of California, Irvine. He is the author of two critical works, *The Style of the Short Poem* and *"Ulysses" and Justice,* and four previous books of poetry. Among his awards and honors are a Eunice Tietjens Memorial Prize, a Guggenheim fellowship, a Paterson Poetry Prize finalist designation, and, most recently, a Whiting Foundation Writer's award.

The University of Chicago Press, Chicago 60637
The University of Chicago Press, Ltd., London
© 1996 by The University of Chicago
All rights reserved. Published 1996
Printed in the United States of America
05 04 03 02 01 00 99 98 97 96   1 2 3 4 5

ISBN: 0-226-56104-6 (cloth)
       0-226-56105-4 (paper)

Library of Congress Cataloging-in-Publication Data

McMichael, James, 1939–
    The world at large : new and selected poems, 1971–1996 / James
McMichael.
        p.   cm. — (Phoenix poets)
    I. Title.   II. Series.
PS3563.A31894W67   1996
811'.54—dc20   96-15122
                                                        CIP

⊗ The paper used in this publication meets the minimum requirements of the American National Standard for Information Sciences—Permanence of Paper for Printed Library Materials, ANSI Z39.48-1984.

Contents

Foreword, by Alan Shapiro · *vii*

The Vegetables (from *Against the Falling Evil*, 1971)

The Artichoke · *3*
The Asparagus · *4*
The Cauliflower · *5*
Herbs · *6*
Corn · *7*
Celery · *8*
Bell Pepper · *9*
Potatoes · *10*

Each in a Place Apart (1994) · *11*

Four Good Things (1980) · *77*

The Lover's Familiar (1974)

Matins · *143*
Lauds · *144*
The Very Rich Hours · *146*
Prime · *152*
Terce · *153*
Lutra, the Fisher · *154*
Itinerary · *156*
Sext · *167*
The Inland Lighthouse · *168*
Nones · *169*
The Great Garret, or 100 Wheels · *170*

The Queen Anne Cottage · *172*
Vespers · *178*
Its Time · *179*
Compline · *182*

New Poems (1996)

She · *185*
Pretty Blue Apron · *188*
The World at Large · *191*

Foreword

Somewhere Isaiah Berlin has written that there are two kinds of people in the world: those who divide the world into two kinds of people, and those who don't. While the world of American poetry is too heterogeneous to be usefully described in terms of any one dichotomy, the recent debate if not the recent practice of American poetry does seem to divide itself roughly into two opposing aesthetic camps: one based in the lyricism of subjective life, the other in the skepticism of the intellect. In the former camp, associated rightly or wrongly with the MFA workshop, we find mostly free verse poems underwritten by an unexamined faith in old-fashioned notions of individual authenticity and self-expression. In the latter camp, embodied most rigorously in the poets associated with the Language school, we find all fictions of unmediated selfhood thoroughly exploded, and subjectivity in general sacrificed on the experimental altar of the indeterminate sign. This dichotomy of course is way too neat. It overlooks the extent to which Language poets such as Michael Palmer and Lyn Hejinian do achieve a poetry of intense though unconventional feeling, even at their most skeptical, or the extent to which poets such as C. K. Williams or Louise Glück write with philosophically informed self-consciousness even at their most emotionally intense. Yet if this dichotomy simplifies too much, it's useful nonetheless in helping us distinguish those poets, who do in fact conform too neatly to one camp or the other, from those who resist identification with either extreme, whose ambition and achievement are precisely to bring together and integrate what in the work of their contemporaries is found mostly in isolation.

Defying all such categories, James McMichael is preeminently such a poet. That his work is often highly esteemed by poets who fall on either side of this division bespeaks the importance and originality of his achievement. Many on the literary left see in his work a rigorous challenge to conventional forms of understanding and expressing subjective life; many in the MFA mainstream admire the emotional and psychological precision of his depictions of individual experience.

The World at Large: New and Selected Poems, 1971–1996 brings together the best of his remarkable work from the last twenty-five years. Early and late, in every volume, from his first two books, *Against the Falling Evil* and *The Lover's Familiar,* through his two book-length poems, *Four Good Things* and *Each in a Place Apart,* to the new work collected here, McMichael demonstrates a breadth of accomplishment few poets in the postwar period can match. What bringing together the best poems from these four books enables us to see is not only the incredible variety of modes and idioms McMichael has mastered over the course of his distinguished career, but the thematic unity from poem to poem, book to book. McMichael's formal and intellectual restlessness is driven by a few obsessions that, far from blinkering his vision, consistently compel the most astonishing insights into the nature of public as well as private experience. Over and over he discovers new ways of approaching the problems that have always vexed and troubled him: the sense of the unpredictable in life as both a source of value and of harm; the desire for immunity from danger, from pain and loss, and the recognition that such desire is itself a kind of danger; the need to impose order upon the world, to make the world amenable to will, and at the same time to acknowledge that the world necessarily eludes the terms by which we try to understand it and control it.

The earliest poems in *The World at Large* articulate these issues indirectly. Poems such as "The Vegetables" from *Against the Falling Evil,* his first book, and most of the poems from his second book, *The Lover's Familiar,* are detached in tone, oblique in manner, employing the spooky imagistic surfaces that were popular among many American poets in the late sixties and early seventies. What distinguishes McMichael's poems from the period style, however, is his fine ear, his energetic and expressive syntax, and an overall formal beauty that controls and specifies the emotional associations that the juxtaposition of images releases. The poem that looks ahead to his more mature and ambitious work is "Itinerary," from *The Lover's Familiar.*

An amazing quest poem in reverse, "Itinerary" moves eastward across America and backward in time, beginning with the poet in the Far West and ending with a seventeenth-century New England Puritan walking in his garden, getting ready to embark upon a journey the poem itself has just completed. Speaker succeeds speaker (Meriwether Lewis, William Bird, Cotton Mather, to name just a few of the personas who inhabit McMichael's voice), as gradually as one landscape and time emerges from others, each one conveying a deepening experience of the natural world that spans the strictly reportorial, the scientific, the mercantile, the religious, and, underlying all of these, the erotic. Taken together, the vocal, temporal, and geographical shifts and transformations enact, even this early in his career, McMichael's keen sense of the fragmentary and unstable nature of identity, composed, as it is, out of a multiple and ever-changing history. Here are the closing lines:

> It comes to me
> that the world is to the end of it
> thinking on itself and how its parts
> gather with one another for their time.
> These are the light, and all the forms they show
> are lords of inns wherein the soul takes rest.
> If I could find it in myself to hide
> the world within the world then there would be
> no place to which I could remove it, save
> that brightness wherein all things come to see.

When the speaker characterizes the forms of light as "lords of inns," he is in effect acknowledging that even the rest his soul now takes is only temporary lodging, a lucid interlude on a journey that, as the entire poem shows, is fraught with violence, uncertainty, and restlessness. When one realizes that the speaker is in fact preparing for the journey that the poem has already enacted, and that the conclusion represents a kind of hopeful prayer, one archaic meaning of the word "itinerary"—a prayer for safe passage made at the beginning of a journey—comes alive. And this revivification in turn further qualifies the speaker's state of grace, suggesting that he implicitly anticipates the dangers that we, as readers, know he will encounter.

I've talked in some detail about this poem because I think it holds the key to all of McMichael's work, for all his poems are shot through with an almost preternatural sensitivity to danger, to the many ways we all are at the mercy of "the world at large" by virtue of our existence in separate, needy, and vulnerable bodies. McMichael's keen sense of being at the mercy of a world one can't control is ultimately connected to his mother's death from cancer when he was a child. That early loss, as he broods upon it indirectly in "The Vegetables" and then explicitly in *Four Good Things,* becomes an emblem of loss in general, a specific instance of a vulnerability synonymous with life itself.

This vulnerability connected to our need for one another is perhaps the most poignant motivation behind McMichael's penchant for anxiously displacing his attention from people and relationships on to landscapes, houses, objects, plans, or systems. The impulse is essentially stoical, a way of pulling back, or desiring to pull back, from what he can't control and what therefore can hurt him: "Because I had to deal with nothing / but a house or houses, I could be / closed off from what they held and have that mean / precisely that they couldn't hurt me." And yet if this displacement of attention originates in fear, it also provides McMichael with an imaginative vantage point from which to better understand the very relationships he fears yet is unable *not* to need, and to place his personal needs and fears within the framework of the wider public world. Over the course of *Four Good Things,* McMichael makes connections between his own compulsion to worry and plan (and by means of planning to create an illusion of control over contingency) and collective forms of social planning, controlling, mapping, that by implication become collective forms of stoicism. What he says, for instance, about the early nineteenth-century English merchants and industrialists is oddly resonant with the more personal, more conventionally autobiographical sections of the poems:

> They were still in that plain geography of
> "things in their places," of bales on
> hoisting-pulleys and in ship-holds and, along the quays,
> the dry white scudding that they lost as waste.
> They were looking for those samenesses that make us feel we've
> broken through to something, through those
> unsure things that happen in a place in time to
> something like our safe impalable and self-sustaining
> plans that are always future.

The phrase "things in their places" echoes what McMichael says earlier about how his conception was coincident with his mother's cancer:

> With my conception, I was virtually
> coincident with cancer in my mother's body.
> To exist is to be placed outside, where there are
> things to fear. My body. Me . . .
> My worrying and fear are notices that I don't
> have a place outside and don't know how to
> find or make one. They are as free of people as a
> garden is, or as a plan.

This passage, in turn, reverberates with what he says two pages earlier about the German and American habit of social and economic planning: "Germany and the United States were planners. Each / consolidated all its worries, tried to organize / the clutter of the unpredictable to make it / go their way. . . . " Of course no culture or individual can eliminate the unpredictable. Nor would they want to. The problem *Four Good Things* obsessively returns to is the troubling recognition that neither individuals nor cultures can do without, nor thrive apart from, the very risks they fear.

Few of McMichael's contemporaries have managed to write as lucidly or as inclusively as he has in this poem about the interdependencies of self and world. The implicit connections McMichael draws through verbal echoes, and the explicit ones he posits and explores, don't represent a monolithic explanation for individual and collective life. He doesn't collapse the distinction between self and society in such a way that society becomes the self writ large and self society internalized. Rather, in the psychosocial vision he develops, public and private experience, self and world, remain distinct yet intersecting, mutually entailing rays of a shared history.

McMichael's habitual displacements of attention are manifested in the more recent work as a preoccupation with space or spacial relations. In *Each in a Place Apart,* his book-length poem about the break-up of a marriage, places and settings provide the terms in which he meditates, the forms through which he feels. They aren't objective correlatives exactly, in that they don't imply a loss of faith in the power of abstractions to articulate emotion. Setting is McMichael's memory machine—he calls up the past he shares with his second wife Linda by means of the places associated with their life together (Southern California), and he attempts to enter more deeply into her life apart from him by imagining as vividly as possible the places that are hers alone, the places in her life that bear no trace of him (England, for example). The emphasis on setting acknowledges and respects, however painfully, her separateness, her independence from his desire to possess her wholly, in his own terms. At one and the same time, it enacts his desire to "join her on / her side of our separate past," and the impossibility of doing so.

The new poems which conclude *The World at Large* are wonderful extensions of this habitual uneasiness and fear. They are remarkably inventive, especially "Pretty Blue Apron" and the title poem, in the way they play with the numbers one through four as metaphors for the problems of being, of individuation, of relatedness and need. As I understand the poem, the numbers roughly represent the following: zero corresponds to the unactualized, the impossible, absence or oblivion, or reality as it is in itself before the mind can think it; one corresponds to any one person, but also what one desires to be at one with; two corresponds to a person other than oneself, or more than one thing or one time, but less than one whole thing if one feels separate and wants to close a distance; three corresponds to progeny from two persons, or all people or the collective; and four corresponds to social practices, institutions, collective habits, or rituals. As categories, the numbers are porous, and unstable, and, like all the forms that we devise "to organize the clutter of the unpredictable," they're mostly inadequate to the materials they contain, or point to, an inadequacy nowhere more apparent than in the way the very lively and unpredictable sentences and the things they express continually overrun the sections for which each number serves as a subtitle. The numbers, in other words, represent another version of the desire for control which the fluidity of life defeats. Like the worrying in *Four Good Things,* the numbers dramatize McMichael's love of maps, plans, systems, as a stay against confusion; and yet in the way it exceeds the numbers that attempt to order it too precisely, McMichael also shows us that he just as deeply loves the world in all its fearful mutability.

One last comment on the way McMichael has organized the book: the interweaving of old and new work, with the oldest coming first, then followed by the most recent, creates an interesting effect in terms of his own presence in these poems. The "I" is absent in "The Vegetables," or rather is the implied but never stated background to the objects he attends to, but he in his own voice is central to *Each in a Place Apart.* The speaker as protagonist is also central in *Four Good Things,* though his attention ranges way beyond personal experience. In *The Lover's Familiar,* the "I" is present only in "Itinerary" and even then it's not the poet we hear exactly but the historical personas inhabiting his voice. Then in the last poems the "I" completely disappears, yet these poems, unlike the earlier ones, are much more meditative, more discursive, and speak more profoundly and directly, not exclusively through the obliquities of metaphor and symbol, of the issues that pervade almost every other poem in the book. Looked at as a single work of art, *The World at Large* has all the social, historical, psychological variety and penetration of a novel and all the formal beauty of a lyric poem.

What we learn from James McMichael's work is to distrust the oppositional rhetoric which often dominates if not the poetry we write then the way we often talk about that poetry. His work is vital because it's deeply skeptical, and deeply felt, lyrical and intellectual, imagistic and discursive, keenly attuned to the socially and linguistically constructed nature of subjective life, even as it broods upon these issues in an idiom and manner that seem unmistakably his own.

Alan Shapiro

The Vegetables

E.L.M., 1900–1951

The Artichoke

She bore only the heart,
Worked at the stem with her
Fingers, pulling it to her,
And into her, like a cord.

She would sustain him,
Would cover his heart.
The hairy needles
And the bigger leaves,

These she licked into shape,
Tipping each with its point.
He is the mud-flower,
The thorny hugger.

The Asparagus

She sent packs of great beasts to pass
Over him, trailing belly-fur and dust,
Bending their nostrils to his frail spear.
This was to toughen him. For what?
Stupidly, like a squirrel, standing up,
Looking here and there, looking to all sides,

He is cut down and taken away.
She can smell him steaming, his crowns
Already tender, his spine giving in.
Now he is threatening to wither terribly,
And slip from the water altogether,
And billow through the kitchen like prayer.

The Cauliflower

Her words clot in his head.
He presses himself to remember
And feels the skin peel back,
The skull bleach, crack, fall away.

All that's left of him is the brain,
Its tissue knotting up to shade him,
The pain of its light pulsing
How to move, how to move.

Herbs

Before fog leaves the scrub-oak
Or the grasses of the downland,
Take dragonwort under the black alder,
Take cockspur grass and henbane,
The belladonna, the deadly nightshade.
Free them as you would a spider's web,
Singing over them: Out, little wen,
                    Out, little wen.
Sing this into the mouth of the woman.

Corn

I am the corn quail.
What I do is quick.
You will know only
The muffled clucking,
The scurry, the first
Shiver of feathers
And I will be up,
I will be in your
Head with no way out,
Wings beating at the
Air behind your eyes.

Celery

The hope with
water is that it
will conceal nothing,

that a clearness
will follow upon it
like the clearness
after much rain,

or the clearness
where the air
reaches to the river
and touches it,

where the rain
falls from the trees
into the river.

Bell Pepper

To find enough rooms for the gathering
The walls go on alone not waiting
For corners but thinking of sleeves
And how the wind fills them and the snow
Fills them and how cold it is without
Fires when there are not enough rooms.

Potatoes

It had been growing in her like vegetables.
She was going into the ground where it could
Do better, where she could have potatoes.

They would be small and easily mistaken
For stones. It would fall to her to
Sort them out, persuade them to stay

Close to her, comforting her, letting her
Wear them on her body, in her hair,
Helping her hold always very still.

Each in a Place Apart (1994)

At school, I was a
squad-leader. I'd gotten enough votes. It meant
I'd wear as bandolier over my white T-shirt
a red cotton sash. It meant I'd say who'd play left field.
She was back in the hospital. My father saw her
every day. Though she was usually about the same,
tonight she was better. He took me to the
Crown Cafeteria, my favorite place to eat.
Waiting for the light so we could cross Colorado,
he said she'd died. The stairs to his office echoed.
Through the front windows we looked out over the street.
I was sitting in his lap in the big swivel chair.
    "But you said she was better."
    "She *is* better. This is better."

The small, pretty woman at the station.
Where would she sit? Eager, tanned and brash, a soldier
followed her to the wide rear seat, I followed too but
stopped, tried not to listen, I was fourteen. Incredibly,
she moved. Could she sit with me? She was on her way
home from her sister's, she'd been there while her husband
closed things up in Fresno, where they'd lived before.
Did I like Utah? She did and didn't, and why.
My answers to her reasons spared me the tight
stultifying fear that I would touch her, her hand was
there but I wouldn't touch it, I could breathe, I managed
even to turn toward her when she talked. We went on to
families, mine first, her questions intimate and long.
She never betrayed it if she thought me young
but she wasn't flirting. I wasn't confused, I knew
right where I was with her: I was lost. It was getting
dark outside and we were hungry. We bought sandwiches in
St. George. Back on the bus, she said she hadn't
slept well the night before, I said she should put her
head on my shoulder if she wanted to. A quick pleased
hum in her throat as she skewed toward me, nestled,
and complied. Past Las Vegas, where she woke a little,
lifted it and then let it rest, her head
stayed on my shoulder. She slept. That was what mattered.
My vigil was to know that I could leave and not disturb her.
She held me just above the elbow with her left hand.

Wanting more and more to thank her and to say goodbye, I
knew she'd sleep beyond my stop and wake and think about me
mostly that I must have left.

My parents had teased that if I ever
caught a fish I'd take it to bed. Warm lakes had
catfish. Trout were the fish I wanted. They were in the
mountains that abided out of view in almost every
Western I saw. In the benign ephemeral first frames with
boardwalks and tethered horses, frontages, a cloudless day,
kill was promised. More alluring were the extras.
They were harried sober people. The women had
children with them sometimes, and of the men,
any one might even then be on his way to rent a
pack train at the stables. This man had started planting
fingerlings in the high lakes six years before. They'd taken.
Having seen good brood stock there, he was heading
back to them now with his mules and tins and would
parcel them out. Until Mike Cady got his car
(he'd be buying it in June and then we'd go),
the *Inyo-Mono Fishing News* had pictures of big
rainbows and browns. They couldn't have been the last.
Above the canyons in the valleys that rose lake by lake,
there were others with the same pearl underbellies,
the same intransigent ways. Some shorelines dropping
headlong toward them through the top clear zones,
it was easy for me to translate into any equal
volume of water the air inside the tall green
handball court walls. Each was somewhere in a given cube.
The water touched their noses, it touched their sides. Hungry,

beautiful and secret, they held to the beryl half-light,
the sunken boulders opaline and faint. Mike and I had brought
sheepherders' bread and a can of black olives.
No one had been in there yet ahead of us over the snow.
Near the top, where the lake was, Mike said he was sick.
He got in his sleeping bag and didn't want to talk.
There was sun left only on the Inconsolables
and they were orange with it and riven, glacier-backed.
I fished a little in the outlet, which had thawed.
How deep the drifts would be at every saddle in the long
profile of the crest. Basins on the other side were
three days from any trailhead. Missing my dad,
I knew I should eat something, I knew I'd be awake all night.

A highway runs the
length of the peninsula. The suburbs overlap.
She lived in one of them and took around with her
her setting. Shops and houses, luminous spring lawns,
streets that led off to places she'd speak French.
Unpunctured by the phrase "One evening" or "One fine day,"
her setting promised it would yield the longed-for.
We met one evening at church, but the adjacent
backyards, the balm of their untold repository
waiting in the dark as, introduced, we
looked at one another, looked away. 1964,
November, but the earth, its different settings for
still other stories, its planes of lines extending and
reversible at any point. Saltflats. An abandoned
tinker's van in a swampy field. The wooded island
upstream from the bridge, the one down.

Nor was it even then too late. I was the
married, reliable sponsor to her youth group,
I had to keep it to myself. Away from her, inside me,
it would suffocate, I thought, if I stayed busy.
My body kept it alive. What if she weren't
there again for a third straight week? I should
want her not to be there. Love meant wanting her to be
comely, prized and occupied, light-spirited, it meant
wanting her not to want me. Another Sunday and she
wasn't there. If I told her, would she want me then?
I couldn't tell her, couldn't not, and did.

I wanted for her sake to undo it,
I asked her to forget. There wouldn't be
time for us since I was married. I'd made her want
another time, when, whole, impossibly together,
we'd rescue my avowal, which was a curse.
Though I asked her not to, she went on
waiting for that time and, by the tree where I
couldn't get away to meet her, waiting
undismayed, heartsick, eighteen.

When she ushers at an outdoor evening concert,
I meet her at the side gate. She can stay until ten.
On a bicycle to the eucalyptus grove, she brings her
This England book. She'd been there with the
parents of a friend one summer and wants to show me
London and the Cotswolds, Chester, Blenheim, Rye.
Standing on a felled tree, she pulls my head to her shirt.
Every time for us is a rehearsal for September 8th
when we'll say good-bye. We know we'll write. We write
daily for a year. By thinking that on her way
south sometime to see her grandmother I'd have
two hours with her in Union Station, I hold on.
My walk toward her from the car, her seeing me, her
face and how she'd feel against my chest. Of those
last minutes with her there would be a first, then others
after it, their series welling at my wrists and temples.
She'd let go of me, she'd turn to get her train and we'd have
lived it, we'd remember, it would have to be enough.
She writes that she is changing schools. Should she be
four hundred miles away or only sixty?

Surprised at my surprise that I can say
    "Sid Kitrell's house . . . , Tim Shirley's . . . ,"
she's next to me in the car, I'm showing her where
I'd lived, Lucile's, my father's office, with her
next to me she leads me to connect for her as many
disregarded things as I can say, I say them,
make them her things too and Pasadena
street by street is comfort, it's Linda and comfort,
the afternoon awash with her sure care.

It wouldn't be fair to us for her to lie.
Whole days with me have made her days alone much harder.
I'm not to worry. She just needs to get her
strength back. It helps that she can see me in a month.
She thinks she's sharing me, thinks I'm not
all hers. I can't tell her otherwise and
stay married. We write and phone, I keep seeing her.
There's no good way out.

In my stupid arithmetic, we're
outnumbered, she and I, by my wife and two sons.
Barbara doesn't notice any change. We visit her
parents. Her dad and I go fishing. Bobby's in school.
Linda never asks me to leave them, never says she'll
leave me. We promise only that we'll meet next
week again at Vicki's or at Chuck's. The quick
assurances each time, we're fine, it's again been
less than too hard and here we are. Then always
rapture and protestation, doubt, self-doubt, and
lingering, the future that we're sure we've lost
forever there for us in our clothes on the cold floor.

Back with her family the second summer,
she guides foreigners around the campus,
learns from the escort to an Argentine the little
training she would need to do his job.
Letters are her way to show us both that she can
stay busy, nothing in what she does too small to tell.
How she's doing she gauges by where it doesn't
hurt her to go. To be somewhere we'd been and not be
hurt by it is to love me well, to be glad it's
me she loves and not someone she could both
love and be with. Because she'd looked for me there
one Sunday when I didn't come, the quad is hard.
So's the amphitheater, the benches under the oaks.
After breakfast once, she walks to Lagunita.
At the far shore, children with balloons run on
ahead of their parents. The water is still.
She sits for a long time on an old railroad tie.
Everything about the morning is quiet and bright.

At eleven she'd been mother to her mother's twins,
was Queen of the May at twelve. Her parents drank.
She wasn't to go to bed without saying
goodnight to her mother. Every night her mother
told her she was bad. Her mother was right. She was
bad not to love her mother, which her mother knew.
Her mother also knew that she loved other people.
Did she love them so that she could hurt her mother?
It hurt no one for her to love places.
Her favorite story was about a place two children
went to meet a third. It was a walled place with
tall trees. The door to it was overgrown because
they weren't supposed to go there, no one was to go
inside, that world so gray with disaffection
it looked dead. They tended to the plants and borders,
listened always for some grown-up who might find them out.
Someone was there. As she came toward them she smiled.
The third child said
        "It's mother—that's who it is!"
and then again
        "It's mother!"

"A picture that scares me has gone through my mind
several times in the last few weeks. I see myself
sitting in front of a fire and being very lonely,
needing you very much. I have a husband and children
and feel very unfulfilled. You aren't near enough so I can
see you and Margie is far away, in fact the house is
out in the middle of hundreds of leafless trees,
the leaves are on the ground. It's absurd in some ways
because I could never live that far away from
other people. I can't imagine children who wouldn't
keep me from being lonely. The husband is a dolt.
I wouldn't marry a dolt but I must not have found
anything as good as you and me again and that scares me."

She hates loving to be with me, I with her.
I have angina, cancer of the testicles.
Staggered against my pulse to their own odd beat,
spasms in my left eardrum last three or four
days at a time. As they slacken, I count how many
breaths I can steal before the next one pops.
She lets me tap them out on the back of her hand.
I can't get them right. My finger is late.
I have to keep saying
      "No, not then"
and, still alone with them, start over, thinking we're
both crazy, how can it matter and could she maybe
hear them with her ear against my ear?

She writes that yesterday had been very good.
Carol wanted to talk and so they went to the beach.
The ocean was a wonderful, stormy color.
She knows it would have to be a quick look but would I
do something for her? Would I come see her room on
Friday at nine? We won't be seen. She promises.
Everyone would be gone then and I could cross the
church parking lot to her back door. That's where she is now.
The orchids are next to her on the bench in the sun.
A jay is covering something up with leaves.
I have ten minutes of class left, she writes, and am
probably not thinking about her. She wants to know what
page I'm on in the book we're both reading.

Everything is in the way. If it's just
Barbara and the boys who stop us, I see them
anywhere, in common bodies, there are calculable
miles of them between our house and Linda, between it and
Linda in five years. She and I will be
through then and I'll go on seeing, I'll think
daily not to drive somewhere we'd been. Even as I
wait for her here and know that maybe in the next
look behind me I will see her car, it's still
Holmby Park, triangular, genteel, its huge trees
hiding what would show in section if they were
split from the top and didn't fall, if they were split
again and didn't and again until they weren't
dark anymore inside. The darkness is their store of
times they've been seen as backdrop to a face seen
one last time. It won't be today we'll add to it.
We'll walk a little and then go to Vicki's,
we'll come back later for the other car.

I know I'll lose her.
One of us will decide. Linda will say she can't
do this anymore or I'll say I can't. Confused
only about how long to stay, we'll meet and close it up.
She won't let me hold her. I won't care that my
eyes still work, that I can lift myself past staring.
Nothing from her will reach me after that.
I'll drive back to them, their low white T-shaped house
mine too if I can make them take her place.
I'll have to. I mustn't think her room and whether if by
nine one morning in a year she will have left it,
sleepy, late, remembering tomorrow is New York,
her interview with UN General Services a
cinch to go well. What I must think instead is Bobby's
follow-through from the left side. He pulls my lob past Geoff,
who's bored. Shagging five soaked balls isn't
Geoff's idea. I tell him he can hit soon. He takes his time,
then underhands the first off line and halfway back.
Ground fog, right field, the freeway, LAX. She has
both official languages. For the International Court,
"The Registrar shall arrange to have interpreted
from French to English and from English into French
each statement, question and response." Or maybe it will be
Washington she'll work for. On mission to a new
West African republic, she might sign on with
Reynolds, Kaiser, Bethlehem Steel. They needed Guinea's

bauxite for aluminum, manganese from Gabon,
their dealings for more plants and harbors slowed by lengthy
phonecalls through Paris, When there were snags, she'd
fly there that same afternoon, her calendar a mix of
eighty hours on and whole weeks off. There'd be
sidetrips to England by Calais and one aisle
over from her on the crossing, by himself,
the man I saw this week I fear she'd like.
He'd have noticed her before they cleared the dock, she'd been
writing something, left wrist bent toward him, the card almost
filled, now, with whatever she'd been telling someone else.
She'd start another, the address first. Eased that he'd
sense it in his shoulders when she stood to leave,
he'd keep himself from looking, it was much better
not to look, he might not interest her, better
not to be left remembering how she looked.
Dover. He'd follow her to the train and sit
across from her, apply himself convincingly to his four
appointments and their dossiers. After she'd make
notes to herself from a bed and breakfast guide,
from *The Guide to the National Trust,* she'd put the books
back in her hemp bag. He didn't mean to be
nosy, he'd say, but was she going to
see some country houses while she's here? Comfortably,
she'd tell him which ones. Though he knew them all, he'd be so
taken with her that he'd lose what she was saying,
he'd undergo the list and ask if she'd be
hiring a car. She'd pick one up tomorrow in
Hammersmith and then drive west. Would she have
dinner with him tonight? She'd say she'd like that:
she was booked at the St. Margaret's, off Russell Square,
could he meet her there at seven? When she'd close her eyes,
her head against the cushioned wing of the seat,
he'd think her managing to rest was not so much a
carelessness to his attentions as that she wasn't vain.

She wouldn't catch him watching if he angled his look
away from her toward the window, in the tunnels
especially he'd see reflected in its glass her gradual
full outline as she breathed. There would be time all
evening to talk. He'd tell her then about his
uncle's place in Surrey where they'd both be welcome,
its rubble-stone and leaded casements, tile, an east
loggia to the lawns and wooded slope. He'd loved the
kitchen garden as a boy, the path there, silver
lavender and catmint borders, an oak-doored archway
framing for him on chains above a well the twin
coronas of roses in the cool damp light.

Nothing is more delicious or remote: after
dinner some night in our own place, I bring her tea.
I can't tell her that. Telling it would say these
meetings of ours are far too little, it would hurry us
beyond them to the time we give them up. And there is
Easter. Over the long weekend, my wife takes the boys
away with her to see friends. We have four days,
more than we'd ever hoped for or think we'll have again.
We don't know what to do with them. Why can't we
save them for later when we aren't this close to having
just what we want? Locked in their icy cirques,
the lakes in the Sierra are three months away,
we can't go there. Of if we did go, what if the car failed,
what if we had to leave it to be fixed? Though safe is
my way, not hers, she doesn't argue. We have
sand-dabs in San Clemente. We drive to Oceanside.
Back at Chuck's, I'm afraid to turn on the lights.
Friday is all right but it seems best that she go
home to the Y. I go home. A few days later
I tell her on the phone I'm leaving them.

To get away from the house to see her
I'd kept pleading work. The library at school was
quieter, I'd said, the kids weren't there. It had served,
though they weren't troublesome or loud. Now, I sit them
next to one another, tell them I'll be moving
away for awhile, that I'm going to live
somewhere else. Nothing from Geoff, from Bobby
instantly a chuckle and smile.
    "Are you happy? Why did you laugh?"
    "Because now we won't bother you when you have to write."

My wife is taking it well enough.
If there's another woman she doesn't want to know.
In LA, where no one knows us and would tell,
I rent a studio above a garage. Linda moves
out of the Y to the front unit of a duplex.
She's at the Ambassador for Bobby Kennedy's
victory party the night I leave. Dumbfoundedness,
one more impossible cortege, but she can come
over now, I can go see her, summer, our walks up the
fireroad in the last light, rabbits and even
deer sometimes across the reservoir on the grassy fans.
We go to the store together. There's time for
movies, now, and double solitaire. We wrestle.
She cuts my hair one Saturday outside her kitchen.

I have to teach again that fall and move back
down to Laguna. The days alone are less baleful,
they're just for a year. No one ever stops by,
but when she drives down on Thursdays after class
I meet her at the Tic-Toc Market. My apartment's
little more than the bed, and we can't wait.
Safe-harbored, whispering, with always more to tell,
we stay put, the dark catching up with us each week
until it's there in our first hour. From upstairs,
the muffled after-dinner clatter. Somebody's phone.
We start over at her knee, we're slower, the prolonged
fine sadnesses we'd hoarded from the years before
slow to give way and slowing so that only after
nothing for awhile does what we're doing take us
not toward her finishing again (or not right now) but
anywhere we've missed, her ribs, only the lightest
grazing of them, down and forward, not too far
nor too far back again across, each furrow
closer by its width to that last ridge below the pliant
dominating compass of her breast. We're being
pulled, of course. She hasn't stopped me. She won't.
At its outermost, her body's what she touches with.
It isn't long before she's moving too. Our skins
poised for the next just barely altered place, we're
thread-like stalks, light-running, sheer, our tiny leaves
flush with the basin's wide paved curb. It's still

gate-piered courtyard, ashlar dressed, a balustrade.
From jets above the circular pool alcoves,
water, its affection for an always lower point
tight-channeled in the iris rills, then underground,
the land dropping away through poplars to the dell.
Damp peaty banks easing to the full pond-hollow,
I'd never married, she'd been born to someone else.

Souls. Unconsulted, wet, they're given
breath to, they breathe, there's no time out, they can't work
trades for another's chances, can't sort through their own from
afterwards to write them as they'd have them be.
In the book of all-knowing, the parenthesis
before one's year of birth is there as shield against
the years amassed outside it. It would have taken less than
one of them to have broken through, a moment only,
change with his first moment or with hers that moment you
yourself broke through the cervix and you're either,
this cartoonist walking past you to his car
or a bonneted and aproned wayside gossip slumped
forward on the low stone wall. She isn't wanted
back at the house for hours and hears firsthand what the
kitchenmaid had told her Rose had seen. They were mostly
clothed, Rose said, and on their knees, atremble, Miss Letty
bracing herself in front on both shoulders.
The wood was its long hilltop strip, their quarter of it
dark, unfrequented. Rose had passed absently
across the lane, not down along it and around.
Quiet enough to let her see them first,
she'd pretended she'd seen nothing and was on her way
she couldn't say where. Disheartened, nervous, cold,
they'd recomposed themselves, said what they could to comfort,
taken their separate ways back. Rose, a talker,
knew something now that doomed them. They would be watched.

It had been hard enough already not to hate
their differences in station. Willfully, for months,
Letty had seen him each late afternoon when he carried
back from their daytime storage off the hall
the library's electric lamps. Then last week she'd
timed it wrong, had caught him in his green and yellow livery
groping about under the big table with the plugs.
He wasn't angry, she could tell, because he'd had to
keep himself from smiling. But she'd learned they didn't
fit here anymore. Since their dizzying
unthinkable espousal, the only places common to them
had been places they'd hid. Withy Copse was safest
but it left less time. Nearer, there were stands of hazel, ash,
the thicket halfway to the upper farm. Now that
Rose knew, the intervals afforded them by trees were
closed, they couldn't reach them unseen. Their mischance was
thickness. They had parts that blocked the light.
Knowing each other's schedule to the quarter hour,
each guessed where the other was and stayed away.
As what seemed to them at first no more than caution
stretched into weeks, their smuggled letters feigned
new dispositions of the heart that neither of them
credited or would deny. He wrote that it had
hurt him for a while to know he wouldn't touch her
ever again, but that was over: this way was simply
best for him. And for her too, she answered,
looking for a glimpse of him across the lawn.
In their counterfeit accord, the letters stopped.
Had she stopped wanting him? He couldn't tell.
From overlays of being seen that, never touching, hovered
just at the skin, they'd now pulled back through
veins and tissues to their deep recallings.
His brooding often passed its twin from her midway.
Their jealousies were interdictions. Neither dared
ask about the other. Both feigned wanting to hear.

So well kept was their secret now that each was left
unsure that there was anything to hide. Whatever
rumors there were had not cost him his position.
He took another. Letty stayed. Between them,
indeterminate and nothing-wanting, numinous, that
angel they'd made, the child she'd never carry.
Nothing had happened that last interrupted time. He'd
heard Rose, turned and seen her go. Because he'd only
started to be through just then but wasn't through,
the egg had not been visited by sperm. Earlier,
it had divided from its flooded lymphoid sac,
the threads around its spindle pairing off, dividing,
ready for division once again if through secreted
mucus and the one canal one swimmer
made its way there. Instead, the world was full.
Though Letty had made room for him, there wasn't room for
microfilaments and microtubules, foci, any
orderly partitioning that meant the cells would do
one thing or other but not all. So that instead of
changes that foretold a break within it, there was still
the same bright plenum as before, the interbedded
limestones and clays, escarpment, camber, dip, an
east-draining valley, its assemblages of quarried stone,
its souls. Within the one intelligence of how they'd fare,
the landed and their tenantry were one. What hadn't
changed for them, what couldn't, was the one light of all
possible lucks and bodies. There was the one filled light.
Engendering, diffuse, it went on drawing out
along with itself to their utmost sides all things that
enter into composition. However tardy, we were
latent there ourselves, Linda and I. The one time it's thrown,
each of us has his and her own fatally-obtained number.
The lot that falls to any couple might have been ours.
To the history of marriage and divorce, we hadn't been
born yet, our births were forestalled. Class wouldn't do us in.

Neither would faith. We'd be subject to only the most
genial of prohibitions. Though I couldn't join her on
her side of our separate pasts, we weren't to be
lost to the world as lovers are who in their longing
die or go mad in patience and alone. Which
shirt she'd wear, our pounds-to-dollars ledger, her lost stamp—
light's traverse of all surfaces would show these too.
We'd face a butcher's window once we'd parked.
The high street would be almost empty.
Since from the millrace and the bridge we'd set out
left across it for a tussocky far slope,
that parish was our quitclaim, it had already
ministered to us from its reserves. For as many
hours as all its parts are by themselves,
setting is the chance that something good might happen.
It's entire for that time, no person's there to see as
different and overt the single gateposts, single
free- and leasehold fields. The park wall, its fallen coping
thatched over in a growth of nettles. A twig-bearer's
strong straight flight. Some tofts. Five rushlit cottages.
The places on the ground between the trees.

Except when there's fog,
we can see from our long front window the huge
supertankers and the half-day boats. There are California
gray whales in the winter. I'm through writing by
lunchtime usually if I've gotten a good start,
and on afternoons I'm not at school, there's
reading to do. When I'm at my best with it,
its phrases are as much in league as I want
things for us to be. When I follow to the letter first
this phrase, this one, and now this and this,
they feel looked back on from a time so ample
that whatever has been hoped for is made whole. I'm not
married now. Linda's not alone. I'd gotten almost
used to it the other way. Before, the five or so
hours a week we'd managed for ourselves meant
all the rest were double. Wherever I was, I'd
double it by thinking Linda, it was those places
she was that I should be too. She'd made there be
more for me than what was at hand. I'd come to
need more. There'd never be time, never anything
ahead of us but more hiding. I needed scenes in which
place itself was perfectly the only thing that took place.
Though "the lake would not be so good a painter
if it did not first paint me," I wasn't there to turn
the obviousness of any hill or rock inside.
Air had allowed a range of bodies to crowd it out.

Of those the wind played with, few were irritable.
All could enlarge the earth's surface by as much as themselves.
Lines that might otherwise have shown led in from
maritime and inland floors. Each river was at once
everywhere in its watershed. With their boughs and sprays
touching and interlaced, looms of vegetation reached
continuingly into their own pasts for more shade still.
No two movements were the same, nor no two leaves.
Measure was kept waiting. "What ails thee?" didn't
have to be asked.

She'd loved it when at fourteen she'd gone to school in
Switzerland. Her mother wasn't there to read her mind.
In curlers and quilted robes, the girls had smuggled
leftovers up the back stairs. They'd gotten to go skiing.
She could see Evian across the lake after a good rain.
Though she'd had to go home when the year was over,
she was learning French. It had let her feel she could be
good at something, that her mother was wrong. While she'd
waited to be loved and wasn't, there'd been at least
French for her, as it would be there for her later while she
waited for me. Now that she's finished her
degree in French, she wants to be in diplomatic service.
We're on the wrong coast. She starts translating Sand's
Histoire de ma vie. She takes a part-time library job
and finds the work's all right.

Our house is a winter rental. Each June, we
store everything we don't take with us in the camper to
Idaho and Montana. It's two full days' drive with
desert much of the way, then farms. Only in the
last half hour, past Ashton, up the hill, are there
logging roads and lodgepole, spruce and fir.
It agrees with us to be outdoors all summer.
I'm shameless about how much I want to fish the broad
wadeable meadow streams. The new mayflies can't
lift themselves from the surface film until their
wings dry. When I watch them drift down over the slack water,
disturbances are rocks sometimes and sometimes fish.
Linda does needlepoint and crossword puzzles. She keeps
checklists of the flowers she finds on her long woodland walks.
We do our wash in town and play cards in the hotel lobby.
We have time to read. By August, there are berries.
A six-pack of Grain Belt beer is ninety-nine cents.
Friends have a ranch with acres that stretch back through
bottomland to their mountain pasture. The old
Hodges' place is vacant. They ask us to stay.
In the upstairs bedroom under the cottonwood,
it's almost dark when it clouds up late in the afternoon.
We find cancelled checks in the homestead down by the creek.
Lots are for sale. In our fifth summer there, we buy one.
A contractor frames a house for us which I have
six weeks to enclose. I want to be, but I'm not

good at it, it doesn't please me at all when my rip-cut
splinters the cedar batten, I miss the stud
completely with a second nail and I throw things and scream.
She can't stand it when I'm like this. But though she has to
leave sometimes and not come back for hours, the work gets done.
We drain the pipes, hang shutters, close the place up.

She wants more time to herself once we're back home.
So she can be alone there from noon on, I stay away.
It's harder to work. My journal entries circle.
Unless I stop writing them about our chances,
we don't have a chance. It seemed much better
last week than this. Am I too upset to tell?
I ought to keep myself from making resolutions.
She'll have to see I'm on my own to want me back.
For her, it's day to day. Now that she's doing
graduate work, she has people to speak French with.
Some of them are men. There's probably one she looks
forward to seeing, as she doesn't me, and why
should she, my explosions are her mother's, my having made her
wait those years was what she was used to from the two of them.
In my not leaving Barbara and the boys to be with her,
Linda could again be hopeful, I was being her
parents again, who'd maybe this time give. That was our luck.
Alternate Fridays had sustained us in it, we'd been
together in thrall to the occasional late
Sunday afternoon. She's given all that up as hapless.
Being mated, having me as her mate: it comes to
nothing for her, nothing would be hers to move
away from if she moves from me. Though I
might have left them sooner if she'd asked,
I'm the reminder that she didn't. I tell myself I'll
meet someone else, that I'm companionable after all.

On the weekends, if she's staying home, I drive
up into the hills. Though I'm not any
abler than I was last month to let her go,
I'm practicing. For minutes at a time, a book
holds me away from her and I'm alone.
Her classes keep her busy. We go on bumping
into one another in the kitchen, we share the car.
It isn't until Christmas that she thinks we're all right.
She asks me to come with her to a party.
We're talking more. There are our nightly
little deaths again, and our trips to Westwood.
We watch *The World at War* and *Upstairs, Downstairs,* golf.
Bobby and Geoff are with us every third weekend.
We make a treasure hunt for them in the lot next door.

She gets her M.A. Since she's still working
part-time only in the library, we have
whole summers in the mountains. She plants an alpine
rock garden with a wall and pond. But like going again to
Europe, where we'll stay for a year, whatever she does proves
daily to her that she's waiting. If she'd gotten a good
job by now, or if she'd sold a book, it would be as much
her schedule we were on as it would mine. It's not that way.
A man in Michigan will do an essay she's translated
if she gets the rights. He should have asked for them
himself, the publisher in Paris tells her: she isn't a
millionaire, is she, that she can pay for them on her own.
I want there to be the respite for her of where we are,
am nervous about it too. Without her French and Italian,
I'd be lost. The skylight in our flat is a hatch that opens.
Standing on a chair, my head above the level of the roof,
I see the whole north slope of our deep transverse valley.
We buy duty-free a radio that picks up Munich.
When they go out alone by shortwave into the first
overture to *Leonore,* the violins are
major, tentative, their slow five rising notes a clear fine
pencil of rays over the Tyrol and the high cols.
There are caves below the ridge where Partisans had
hidden from the Fascisti. In the summers only,
goatherds stay there now. So do trekkers caught in storms.
The peasants pay with sandals, sausages and wine

when they come down to see a doctor or for tools.
Disliked and well-to-do, a bachelor, the baker tends at
four each morning to the ovens and the tubs of dough,
then stands outside his shop all day in the blind street.
A black-bordered poster there tells that someone has died.
It's November. On a terraced plot a third of the way up,
bells from the other side are faint enough that what
wind there is must be from the lake. Crossing the
river again on our way back over the old bridge,
lights at the field are on already. I have to be
goalie in our pick-up soccer game or not play, I'm
bad with my feet. Though we have the place here until March,
she thinks that she'll go back to Paris, she'll canvas the trade:
there has to be something she hasn't found that she can try.
She doesn't want me to come with her. Having someone
caring how it goes would make it worse.

An editor in London tells her that he needs to have
translated from the French the third of a
six-volume history. A donor to the press had
murdered the second volume, the reviews had said.
Looking for someone new, they like Linda's sample from it
very much and want the rest by Christmas.
There's room in our flat for each of us to work.
We won't leave for months, but I'm already
missing every Pont Street Dutch facade. These were
her places first, she brought me to them, they were her best
prospects half her life ago, now they've delivered, she has a
book to do, she's happy, it's there to see, I want to
fasten inside me in its sum the way our mews looks,
want to learn by heart which buses take us where.
Twice through the outer boroughs the river bears
west a little, even. Islanded, embanked, it's still
tidal there, the wakes below its balks and pilings
hard to make out. Of the towns in sight of it upstream,
the smaller are set back the widths of churchyards.
It's tree-lined for a field or two on one side only.
From far enough above to show each turn,
reaches of it leave thumbs and bays in the flint gravel.
Tracts of barley and the bright coarse grasses fit
irregularly along it over the floodplain,
the mouths of its feeder-creeks hidden in green flags,
a single cream-white camas spearing

up through the ferns to the tip of its tall sheaf.
I've been restless for her for almost an hour when I
hear her come in. She'd had a good time swimming.

"The sun was shining through the roof into the pool."

The original she's working with is
lazy and gnarled, there's at least as much
editing to do as there's translation. She has each
morning for it, and new purpose, notebooks, her Larousse.
Even when she stays at it into the afternoon,
we still have time for an outing, it's light until nine.
She reads to me on the drive that "the pond will be a
happy one for its lilies if it has near it
some wooded rising ground to shut it in,"
and from the summerhouse on stout oak posts we see
a clover meadow, fields, the chalk escarpment,
then pass the staging for the seed-trays on our way out.
Inside a row-house at the end of the small village,
the double sound of a door meeting its frame and latch.
Weekenders live here now, and a few widows. There's a rep for
industrial motors too, an estate agent, a diver whose
job it is to repair pipeline in the North Sea.
Through a gate she has to close, a young girl leads a pony.
Lorries sweep the grasses back on both sides of the deep lane.
The few last isolated showers have stopped. A man comes
out to brush the rain from his hydrangeas. We're home by dark.
After dinner, a short walk, the BBC, then going to sleep
next to her and waking, her being there to touch. Bobby's
Bob now. He flies over for our last few weeks, flies
back again when we fly to New York. Though we're in
transit for the summer, she averages her two

pages a day. We don't know it yet, but taken up with
work and friends and travel, we'd for the first time ever
forgotten where we were in the month. She's unaccountably
sanguine about the letter waiting for her at home.
It tells her that the donor has found out and won't
have it that he's been passed over. The press is
sorry and embarrassed. It will of course by
all means pay her for her time.

After five years of saying it, it became a
joke with us that we'd have a baby in five years.
We're waiting for the EPT. Sitting as far
away from it as she can and still be home, she wants
me to be the one to read it. I'm surprised how
glad I am. Her not being glad lasts half an hour.
She'll work for the library until she's due in June.
The baby does its tours inside her. When we put the big
headphones on her tummy, it seems to hear.
Her doctor tells her to cut down on salt, her
blood pressure's high. We buy a stethoscope and cuff.
She tells Linda to quit her job and go to bed.
The salt-free cottage cheese is cardboard, but it's
not working, nothing is, I can wait until she's been
resting for an hour before I take it, it doesn't help.
Since her diastolic number's always high, it's of
course high when she sees the doctor: she'll be in the
hospital tomorrow morning if we don't change
doctors tonight. La Leche League has two it recommends.
The one who calls back asks everything. If she were
his wife, he says, he'd want her in the hospital.
We're too frightened to sleep. I hold her. I fall off
only when it's almost light and by then the
birds have started. It makes her cry to hear them.
When she's admitted to the ward, they hook an
IV up to her that hurts her hand. On the vacant bed

next to her, there's a tray with a syringe and drugs:
if she goes into labor she might have convulsions.
They tell us on Monday that the baby wouldn't be able to
breathe yet on its own, on Wednesday that it could
suffocate inside her, her placenta's shutting down.
They'll do another amniocentesis in the morning,
they'll take the baby in the afternoon. She and I are such
cases by now that I think they'll lie, they'll want to
quiet us for the birth by telling us the baby's lungs
are ready, that stranger things have happened in three days.
A nurse comes in and says the baby's lungs are ready,
let's go to prep. Since Linda can't have it
naturally, it matters all the more to her that she at
least be awake. She'll get to be. Both doctors
promised me this morning that she'll have a local,
it's up to them. I get scrubbed. Everyone's in greens.
Down a corridor, away from me so I won't hear,
the anesthesiologist is talking to her doctors,
who are very intent. The scene breaks up. Her doctors
don't have to tell me, I know already, I want to
hit them, I say I'd promised her because they'd promised,
I'd told her she could be awake, that I could
be there with her. Stop it, you can't let her
see you like this, her pediatrician says.
She's partly sedated. I tell her I'll be waiting
right down the hall. From another room than hers, a
baby, a first cry. I have to hear it or not listen too for
our baby, Linda's asleep, she can't. If it's from
her room now that I'm hearing something fainter,
someone should tell me soon. I believe the nurse who says

    "I can't tell you *what* it is, but it's really good."
    "How is Linda?"
    "They're sewing her up now, she'll be fine."
There's no reason not to believe her, Linda's
not going to die, she's not going to die or have to

hate it that she didn't, her baby's all right, we haven't
killed it by not changing doctors. It won't have to be
breathed for by a machine. Almost a month early, he's a
wonder to the staff at five pounds ten, he's Linda's doing,
she should be proud of him, she'll nurse him and she'll heal.
I can buy her now the blue- and white-checked gingham
mother and baby rabbit. I can buy her a robe. He comes
home with her after the weekend. The two of them feel so
hallowed to me that I'm slow to tell it hasn't worked
out for her at all. She writes an essay about it.
His having been taken from her early means she failed.
Bodies are bodies. They know things, they have their own ways.
She could have done it if she'd gotten the chance. Her doctor
didn't want Linda caring how things went. That had to be
her job, not Linda's. She'd gone on to say it almost
proudly of Linda at the last:
        "This little girl would be fine if she didn't have a brain."
It's a long essay. I recognize everything but me.
Not her antagonist, exactly, I'd been another
thing she'd had to worry. Whenever I'd taken her
blood pressure, she'd felt blamed by me if it was high.
Each crisis had been hers to deal with by herself.
Too busy or aloof to find her a better doctor,
I'd taught my classes, read, worked on my poem.

She's at the mirror.
I need to get behind it to the aspirin,
do so, close it.
    "Goodness you wake up with a lot of headaches."
    "Sorry."
    "Don't be sorry, I'm sorry for you."
Surprised that it turned out like that, and
hating her, hating what I'd heard in my own voice,
I get out of her way. From the privacy of
brooding on it in another room, I hear what she meant:
"Congratulations. As good as you are at headaches,
why settle for so little, why not work up a
malignancy of some kind?" And I remember that
yesterday, when we were getting in the car, she winced.
She's always twisting her neck or back or something,
so I didn't ask her "Did you hurt yourself?" but
    "Did you hurt yourself again?"

Impatience, most of all. She tells me that what
she wants when she's impatient with me is that I be
patient. Why am I so upset? Maybe because it's
time to be upset, how should I know,
    "I can't stand the way these fuckers drive their cars."
She tries not to watch me, has been seeing me
rave like this for twelve years and still isn't
used to it. I'm cooler now and look over at her.
Wanting to see at least the disguise of a smile,
I put my hand on her leg. She goes on looking
straight ahead at nothing, keeps it up for another
ten minutes. Domestic farce. Filler. Too little of the
exceptional in what we do from day to day as the
same two people. She knows me too well, each of us
knows too much about the other. Impatient for some
change in the other's nature that we think won't come,
we pout and blow up, dissemble, vex, forgive, go
on with it into the next instances of our
wishing we lived alone.

I want her sense of me to be wrong, want there to be
more than she sees, or something better, she reminds me
too much of what I can't do. The way she has of being
right about me is power. I can tell she thinks I'm distant.
I won't give in, I'll prove to both of us that I'm not.
Talking will distract her. I don't force it,
don't try to sound too cheery. But I'm telling her things I
wouldn't have—I'm saying them badly, distantly,
maybe even on purpose. She asks me
　　"Is it me?"
　　"No."
　　"Then what?"
　　"Nothing."
And I haven't lied, it's nothing, only power.

She likes to be out. Because he keeps us
in more, I help with the baby. She goes out
but wants me to go with her. Though I
go sometimes and like it, I'm sure that she's
insatiable, she's sure that I'm not liking it enough,
and it stays that way. The rest of the time is
mine, the time my writing takes becoming
proper to me, another of my properties, like my
cold hands. I remind her that my work's no fun.
She hadn't forgotten, she says, and neither am I.
It isn't a writer's line, but I say it.

"You want me to be someone I'm not."

"You want *me* to be someone I'm not and I'm
being that person."

As he often does when Linda holds him,
he pulls my fingers to his face. First it's a
nostril that he covers and uncovers languidly
again and again, then it's an eye. He keeps them moving.
If he could make my fingers fit him as her water did,
if my fingers were her water, it would always have been
his doing to have left it there, to have taken it away.
He's invented his Baby Kitties and the Six-year-olds.
Do they do that too? The question makes him sleepier.
As silly as they come, he smiles and goes on dabbing
closed and open, closed and open.

Three years not so much of squabbles as of
routine. Her days in the library, mine at
school and at home. Owen is four. We see friends for
dinner sometimes, talk on the phone to other friends
too far away. We go to Idaho in the summer.
I feel my life is safe because she loves me.
We'd been asleep, twelve years ago, when the
call came about my father. I went downstairs to
answer it, came back, her face asking me who
was it and I told her what. Then her
        "No,"
her arms held out to me from the sheet, her body,
the fathomless spare nurturing
        "O Jimmie"
which I still hear in anything she says.

One Saturday they go with friends to a police
bicycle auction. I stay home to write. By noon, the
Dodgers are on. I turn the sound off and read *Huck Finn,*
which I have to teach. When she comes in with groceries,
she's enraged at me. I'd stayed home to watch a game?
Defensive and chagrined, I can't get her to stop.
She hasn't been this mad for months. I don't cook or
garden with her. I don't dance. Couldn't I not work at least
one morning a week? The auction was fun. She'd kept thinking
how much I would have liked it.

She has to find a new job. It won't
do for her to stay at the library part-time. She's
liked there, the people like her. More and more, it's to
her they come when there are differences. She thinks they
listen to her. Maybe she'd be good in personnel.
She isn't saying it, but she regards as
failures of hers the things she's stayed with. The list goes
far enough back that if before it there'd been
something to draw from now, she doesn't feel it's there.
Having talked all evening, and later, here in bed,
we've been quiet for awhile before she says it.
   "I've got to do it right this time."
"Career" is what I should be hearing. More than anything
else has in our almost twenty years, it scares me
that she means me too.

It's early March. She doesn't know if we've
changed for her, but she's looking forward to June,
she wants me to go to Idaho without her. I'm afraid to.
She'll like it here too much without me and won't
want me to come home. It may already have been
weeks ago that I should have seen it, I can't stop watching,
will we make it or not? She doesn't know. Sometimes she's
hopeful that she'll get the spark back, the one I have for her.
Sometimes she thinks she wants another baby. I
can't let her see I'm cheered. Each time's a chance to
show her that her backs and forths don't matter.
If she feels monitored, it will drive her away.
Something in me touches her for a moment. When she
kisses me at Carl's Jr. while I'm standing in line,
I have to look at her. And if it's for
that moment only that she loves me, I can't hide.

This is more than just our worst fight ever.
She's wanting back the years she's given me, but I'm
right here with her and she can't decide.
It surprises her when I move to an apartment.
Evenings there are the hardest. Going to
sleep once, I don't inhale and wake myself up.
It's the ordinary things that give me the most trouble.
I can't read the sports section. For as long as I've been
opening my office door, she's been in my life.
Though I don't ask to, she says I can come home for
weekends, if I like. Everything seems so
effortless one morning that I tell her
    "You seem better."
    "For now, anyway."
We spend an hour pretending I hadn't slipped.

"You two are a great puzzlement to me,"
our therapist says as Linda hurries out
ahead of us down the hall, late to a meeting in her
new job. She thinks our years together have been her fault.
When I left Barbara and the boys to be with her,
I'd done so much she couldn't bring herself to hurt me.
She knows now that she should have told me no.

I move the rest of my clothes out of the house.
Our fights about money pass. In having to
leave her, I also have to think again the most
forgettable of our outings. Over the years, we'd taken our
bodies along in company to certain places. In
front of me a little to the left, she'd answered "Yes" to
"Two for dinner?" I wasn't thinking, at the time, how I
fit into what she cared about: she fit for me. It comes
back to me now because I have to change it, I'd
gotten it wrong. Normal, expected, there's a brittle
politeness between us when I stop by to pick up Owen.
Below the hem of her flannel housedress, her bare feet.

Four Good Things **(1980)**

for Killarney, to whom it's told

Despise the world; despise nothing;
Despise yourself; despise despising yourself;
These are four good things.

—the Abbess Herrad of Hohenburg

From the McMichaels',
Florence. She passed the Silvers', the Johnsons'.
She was walking to Martello and the bus. She was
the woman who took care of me, and she was going
shopping.
    It was that one time in her life, a Saturday,
an afternoon. She was alone again. Glen was in
Tobruk, or somewhere, in the army, and it was years
after her first husband died, after the early
photograph in Eaton Canyon with the light
about where it was now. She had posed between
two oaks, the heel of each hand flat against them,
sleeves to her elbows, wind, the canyon to one side
dark at the falls where John Muir climbed and found
wild ferns and lilies, villages of wood-rats.
She'd gone only to the falls and come back out to
Pasadena, and the afternoon was just as late
now as it had been then. The sun was low and almost
blocked by the houses south of other houses
facing that way, as ours did. If she started
home again from downtown through the streets,
the houses that she passed between my room and there
were waiting for new tenants, for the doctor, for a
sober infirm neighbor of the Hales to stop
scorching his nose and forelock as he tried to
light his cigarette. If I heard her at the

back door with her packages, I knew that she would
soon start dinner. I'd watch, and she would let me
plead with her about the story of the fire,
give in and tell it, answer what I'd ask.
If I were with her, houses that my father sold
were possible, each at its certain distance from the
vineyard five blocks north. The mountain was absurdly
vertical and dark, and the cars that passed below it
droned in their stupor through the pepper trees.
Stick-piece-place, the stable with the horse and dog
were possible, remembered. Lights were going on in
other kitchens—yours before your parents moved there,
mine at some one time when Florence was with Glen.

How light it was outside was a matter
neither of us thought about. Florence went on
working at the sink. We talked and I kept
busy with the #20 New Connecticut grinder,
turned the crank and sent the bit along in
spirals, like a barber-pole. I took it apart,
followed its channel with my thumb and fit it
back in place securely with the wing-nut, tight.
I did all that again, each step, and we kept
talking. So that when we heard her car
and looked out past the palm tree to the street,
how light it was above the lawns or shrubs,
how far she'd driven or how far he had to drive
was easy, sure, and as composed as any
look she gave me when she came inside. She
talked with us a little, left us to our
interests in the kitchen. We heard his car
and knew that he was glad to be here, glad
for anything we had to tell him, and for her.
He knew she'd live five years. She wouldn't
think about it, would be in and out of

.

wheelchairs, hospitals, assuming to the end
that she was getting better. That made it
tolerable for her, and covered him to work
so thoroughly at what he did all day
that coming home was easy. Dinner. Florence
leaving. Me in bed, asleep. Alone, it was
their time, unless the phone would ring. It would be
for him, some business matter, and would last
indefinitely while she did something else,
arranged the flowers for a still-life sketch,
wrote letters, read. I tell myself that
how they were with one another was as natural
as any hesitation, as their reluctance
ever to let me walk beyond the Johnsons'
or to school. If they were frightened or remote
they lived it over quietly, kept working,
made a long trip up the coast, with me.
I'd go to dinner with them at the Esterbrooks'.
To houses that he'd show on weekends with his sign
staked in the front lawn.

    After she died, his business kept him longer.
Florence had moved away with Glen, and I was
there alone through the afternoons and early
evenings, into the hours when I'd listen
to the radio and wait to hear him drive in,
late. After ten, after my shows were over, I'd
worry every way he might be killed, would give it up
only and completely when his car was there.
With that exhilaration I could put on
all the calmness that I thought he wanted—
pretend to be asleep or answer tiredly
that I was there. I was certainly there, and
had been, hadn't been with him, wherever
he had been. But I didn't hate him for it,

loved him with a dull morose uncomplicated need
that made his days as strange to me as where he
spent them.

That was the sense in which he was the city.
Two years before, he'd stepped off all its lots.
He'd mapped them, called them PASADENA TRACTS and
had them published, found they wouldn't sell.
Stacks of the copies sat there in his office.
He brought some home and I would look for
streets I knew, Paloma, Crary, Brigden Road.
He would be somewhere within his maps at any time—
at the office, mostly, on the phone about exchanges,
tax, big purchases of land for roads and public buildings.
Sales were what I understood. People moved
in and out of houses. Who they were,
what they cared about or did was less insistent
than the fact that they were there at any time for him.
They were his continuity as he was mine.
His listings of the houses up for sale had
pictures that were indistinct. I could make out
one or another, could place it from some
drive we'd taken. I'd see it as it mixed with
others that were occupied and were his business too.
They all made up a neighborhood, were part of that
difference from house to house that showed
more clearly in the mornings when the light
canted around the mountain, lifted, stayed
behind St. Lukes and lifted, took its time,
was fullest on the open porches, in some yards,
on streets like ours that paralleled the mountain,
east to west.

He came home and got me and we drove
west, out Washington. Hill and Lake, Los Robles,
Lincoln, past a school. He told me they'd get

more than it was worth, and he would help them find
another house. Theirs would be torn down so the
school could be expanded. He understood their
wanting to stay. They had nine children.
I wanted it to take us longer to get there.
That way, they might be eating. He'd go to the door,
someone would let him in and they would talk.
I'd wait in the car and watch nothing, think
only about him coming out.

But it wasn't late enough for that. We were
there already, and he made me come in too.
The rooms led off from this one toward the back,
upstairs, along a hallway to the right. Jimmie,
this was Mrs. Damiano. Earlier, on the phone,
he must have told her that I'd lost my mother,
that he felt he ought to take me with him,
sometimes, in the afternoon, like this.
She called her daughter, introduced us and
assigned her to me. The girl was older, poised,
knew what to ask me so she wouldn't seem
indifferent or burdened. I was in love with her.
I managed awkwardly a yes or no, felt overmatched
and homesick. I might have held on if I'd
kept myself from watching her. She would be
someone I could think about. Away from her,
in the car again and going home, I could
construe it some good way—no fantasy, no kiss,
but no ridiculous collapse like this one that was
coming on. She may have asked me what was wrong,
or even left me in a room upstairs while she
went down to say that I was crying, that I
wouldn't tell her what was wrong.

I didn't know. It wasn't a conscious sadness.
I'd made him leave before he'd settled with them.

That didn't mean they'd get to stay. I didn't
care, or if I did I wanted there to be some
retribution. Nothing as clean as the wreckers
piling into it with their great ball. I think of this
now, and place some children there to watch—
not me, who was too old for that, nor any
younger Damiano whom I hadn't seen. Instead,
they'd be from several blocks away and would have
passed it in the weeks it sat there waiting.
They'd have the simple interest in its vacancy
that I have now, but would have wanted to
remember how the upper floor dropped through and
slammed and jostled as the sides were hit
again until it all came down and the trucks
collected it and took it off to burn.

     Two lovers walk out along a road in
Hampshire or Dorset, somewhere in the south.
On a small bridge, they stop without talking.
They are the narrative of their separate marriages
and have begun missing one another already.
Behind them, downstream, on the bank, a teacher
leads her file of students. She is telling them
"I want you to look closely at the river,"
and a few look dutifully and with good will
there, toward the middle, where she shows them that the
weed beds should be cut. She says the flow is
choking around the cups of water crowfoot,
that its surface should be undisturbed and
sometimes even sluggish, cramped, but not like this.
She points out plants along the margins,
the willowherbs and sedges, purple loosestrife, mint.
So they will stay away from it, she makes
each one of them touch once the spiny nettle-leaf.

They squeal and chatter and the lovers are
too far upstream to hear them and the place
between them, on the river, is again
more indivisible than either story. The people
leave within an hour. Even the teacher will forget
the deep unclouded pull below the catwalk
where a thin canal heads out and fills a
water-meadow of the flat. They leave,
and what each takes away is a distinct
autonomy to live and die, feel threatened or
ecstatic, tired, be someone I could come to
care about and yet be impotent to help or hurt
or to have love me with enough brute will to move
inside my need to be immune from things that
matter to me that I can't control.

     Rivers matter to me. I suppose my
carelessness in wading them is a romantic faith
that in a story they are only incidental.
Beyond the body of the suicide, the current
kept and changed its rhythm, hurried and turned
back and under and went on below whatever
rock had made that difference. Complying
evenly again with all the water, it was
nothing like the workers' hearts on seeing her,
nor like her own when she had just let go.
Like her heart now, the river was about itself
the way a vacant house can be about the
Damianos and go on as I would have it go,
not as a prop in an account with general
dispositions of the characters—that they moved
here or there within the city, didn't like the house
and moved away again as one by one the children
left and had their own lives somewhere else.
I'd have it go on as a house and use it as I

use a piece of music, investing it in no
deliberate or exacting way with my retreat from
people and their stories. I never asked my father
what became of them. I know the house was razed.
But I have kept it going on beyond its
natural and even just conclusion, kept it as
possessively as if its being vacant made them mine,
denied their separateness and let me find them
anywhere, in any other house that was as big.
I wasn't looking for them. On the distracted
walks I'd take as a naive voyeur, I had
forgotten them and what the house itself was like.
My finding them unrecognized was that much more
secure and comforting. Because I had to deal with
nothing but a house or houses, I could be
closed off from what they held and have that mean
precisely that they couldn't hurt me. If I
think of all the houses, I don't know which ones
had made me want to take those walks. The old
three-story place on Hill and Mountain was too
obviously dark and gothic, almost funny,
its finials and stained glass like a fairy tale,
a house that some rich lawyer with a lot of kids
might buy and renovate. Others that were set
much deeper on their lots, behind the trees, were more
anonymous. They gave me nothing to oppose—
no walks nor entryways, no lights that I could see
at some one angle as I tried to know if
anyone was there. They were or weren't, and either way
it didn't matter since I couldn't see to will them
back into the back rooms where they would say and do
the things that were their story. I wanted that
suggestiveness that even smaller houses had—

a living room illumined, empty, someone coming
inside from the patio to get the phone.

My mother was dying. I didn't know that,
didn't know why I couldn't be at home when she had
left the hospital to be there. He would
take me to Lucile's and leave me and I'd hate it.
I'd worry that I'd have to stay and go on
living there like one of hers, like Donna, Elva,
Polly, and Dwight. I thought my father knew I
blamed them somehow when my mother died. And, too,
Lucile was his cousin. So when she moved from
Oak Knoll to a bigger place on Holliston,
and when we'd go to see them on the weekends
and would eat there, work together on the house,
when he'd been sick one time just after Christmas
and had slept with her downstairs while I had
stayed awake outside Dwight's room, in the hall,
when Florence even told me what was coming,
told me, as she said, "explicitly" what they would do,
I no more thought about his marrying Lucile
than I had thought my mother wouldn't live.
We moved from Cooley, they were married. Like Dwight,
I had three older sisters and was lonely, vain.
There wasn't any closeness. They had the same
detachment and reserve with one another
that they had with me. The five of us were all
polite enough and did the housework with our
moderate displays of bitching. We saw to it
always that each other's messages got through.
We never interfered, fought only in the
petty ways of adolescents. Donna was loud,
Elva and Polly quiet. If any of the four of them
resented me they didn't show it, seemed

genuinely to like my father, as they always had.
I hated them. I hated Lucile. After that
death, that first one, possibly the last death
ever to surprise me, I'd been surprised again.
I knew I'd left things out when I had worried,
and I hated them for being part of that.
My father seemed as lost to me as if he'd died.
It didn't matter what I felt. We had become
conspicuously a family with any family's
collective will. I'd go on living with them
in a house that they had lived in first.

The mountain north of Pasadena has severe
and angular back canyons where the light is always
unexpected, out of place, too simple for the
clutter of the granite blocks along the creeks.
The slopes have low rough shrubs, some firebreaks.
It rains sometimes, and then the soils wash easily
through Rubio and Eaton canyons to the small
catch-basins and the storage tanks. The bedrocks
tilt toward the west, and so the seepage
drains that way. Along a wall of the Arroyo,
it comes down in springs named Tibbets, Ivy,
Flutterwheel. These are the only steady water,
and the Indiana colony had hauled it out
in tubs and barrels to their lots. They'd cleared
the greasewood from the flats and planted groves of
orange and peach trees, built their houses in the
California Style with battened redwood boards.
Nearer the Arroyo, on its terraces,
they saved a few live oak. They'd have December
picnics there and afterward would walk from
that side, down the bluff. The floor was cool,
and there were sycamore and alder, loose
irregular new channels through the willows.

On the other side, and south, below the San Rafaels,
more oak, the sun. They'd take a new way back.

    Their lots extended east to the Lake Vineyard
Land and Water Company. And as a grudging
compromise between that tract and theirs,
the Central School was built in the dry neat
rows of the orchards east of where they lived.
Excursion parties from the Middle West were taken
mostly with the climate. At the citrus fairs,
the charts and produce showed them that it didn't freeze.
Storms were rare and offered the consoling interest
of a flood in the Arroyo, loud and stupid
boulders the size of safes colliding down the wash.
A new hotel faced south on Colorado. Like the
Ward Block to its right across Fair Oaks,
it was substantial, frame, with dormers and
brick chimneys. Each had its widow's walk
and looked as much like Boston as it needed to.
Someone from Los Angeles brought in a telephone.
He hooked it up in the store on the southeast corner,
rode back downtown and called and asked for
so-and-so, who wasn't there. From that one
crossing, there were fewer lots each month,
new storefronts and more traffic, speculating
boomers and pikers, midnight sales, bands and free
lunches at the auctions. Owners were induced to move
east on Colorado to more eligible locations,
but the cross-streets led through dusty tent-lined
orchards to the chaparral. The boom came back
toward the center and was done. What they'd been
selling was the weather and a place to live, and
that was what was left. As their one industry,
the Novelty Works of Mr. Wakeley went on stuffing
scorpions and trapdoor spiders, horny toads,
small animals and birds. The balance of trade was

not in Pasadena's favor.

But there were jobs. James Scoville kept men doing
rockwork on the banks above his groves. The Arroyo
narrowed there, and so he had them build a
pumphouse and a dam and turn a railroad trestle
upside down between two concrete footings.
This was the central bridge. It crossed to open
ranchland that would subdivide more slowly than the
woodlots on the bluffs. Another bridge, La Loma,
farther south, was taller, with a wider span and
sycamores around its girders. It had replaced the
Johnston bridge and made it easier to sell the tracts.
The wealth of the invisible elite went into homes on
Grand and Orange Grove, Raymond, Nithsdale Rd.,
Arroyo Terrace, Bellefontaine, new bungalows
that looked much less expensive than they were.
In their commissions, Charles and Henry Greene
used common and available materials,
stones from the Arroyo, bricks, a simple flexible
pine frame of 2 × 4s and hand-split cedar shakes,
porches that were railed with the same rough timber
as the posts and beams and trusses and the overhanging
rafters for the roof. Their costs were mostly labor.
They'd show the workers where they wanted
terraces and knolls, what trees and shrubs to save.
A local factory expanded to keep up with them,
and they'd make daily visits there to oversee
the millmen and the carvers or the quality of
lumber that had just been shipped. Their mason did
exactly what they called for on retaining-walls,
the color of the fill, which stone or clinker at what
angle to the rest. Each minor thing they cared about
earned what it had to do with matters that were
not their business. Where the money for a house had
come from, what the Mayor had in mind, or

Public Works, or how the street would look with lights—
affairs like these beyond the garden stayed
accessible, a movement to and from the house
implicit in its horizontal lines. The roof was
long and relatively flat. Beams above the frames of
doors and windows were much broader than the
frames themselves and paralleled the covered
entryways and porches. Even the stairs inside
were less than vertical, each section of the railing
carved from a single piece of teak and joined to
all the other teak—the notched and interlocking
kickplates, the splines and level boards that were
the facing of the well. Their stairs were furniture.
A bench along a landing had the same insistent
finish as the inglehook, the same square
ebony caps for screwheads as the chairs and tables.
Everything showed you how it went together.
A scarf or box-joint, metal straps, continuous
sure banding from the hallway into any room.
There was tile and leaded glass, but it was mostly
wood—mahoganies and walnuts, oak, redwood or
white cedar wainscots, doweled and pegged loose
furniture in teak or birch or lignum-vitae, a smooth
self-lubricating wood that didn't crack. The grain
inside was outside too in rafters and stiff rounded
beam-ends that were oiled and rubbed. They looked
penetrable to light, looked as if they could
absorb and carry it at any single time toward the
one best place inside. Lucile's house on Holliston
was miles from the Arroyo. But it was imitation
Greene & Greene, a less impressive version of their
simplest large two-story frames. Its eaves on
both the north and south reached almost to the
neighbors' lots, lots that for several blocks each way
repeated themselves with slightly different houses.

The man she'd bought it from was still a
pharmacist at Lake and Villa. He didn't know me
and I never spoke to him. He had a massive
tumor on his neck and jaw, and I would be
amazed each time I saw him that he wasn't dead.
Until a year or so before he'd sold the house,
there'd been an organ with the pipes extending to an
upstairs bedroom, probably the room across the hall from
Donna's. There would have been no floor between
the first and second stories, our den and sewing room
a single shaftlike chamber that the sound would fill.
It's just as likely that the floor had been there
all along, exactly as we knew it, with the organ
somewhere else. But of all the rooms downstairs,
only the den could open to the room above it.
With the ranks of pipes along the wall that
backed against the stairs, there would have been
high windows to the south and west, and possibly,
around three sides, a thin railed walk one got to
from the upstairs hall. I might let myself care
more about how well or what he played if it were
clearer to me how the organ looked. If I know
anything about its wood, I know it from the
oak-frame sliding doors between the den and
living room. So if the console had been quartered oak,
the case was walnut—no tracery around the pipes,
the same plain cuts as for the cabinets and counters
everywhere downstairs. How many manuals there were,
or knobs with nameplates for the pitches and the stops,
if the bench was free or fixed, or whether the
pedals for the naturals were strips that flared
slightly in their alignment toward the darker sharps—
the whole clear shape of it in that one place remains as
closed to me as how it worked, as the feeders and the
reservoirs, the valves, the layers of coarse felt between

the double panels of the swell-box; as how the sliders
kept the air below the upper-boards and pipes
and let it go and let it sound the way he
wanted it to sound, the wind inside the pipe
striking against a lip and coming back, contained and
vibrant for the time he kept it there. Its shock to the
air outside the pipe was how it sounded, the way he
wanted it to sound, or as it might have sounded
if the room were larger and the sounds dispersed and mixed
less palpably, went on together with the light or
darkness in the room. There wouldn't have been time
between the sounds to count them to be sure that
nothing of the piece was missing. Nor was there time
for me, at any moment in the sewing room, to know
the changes that the light had worked downstairs.
Not that I would have tried to know, or done much more
than suffer my current fit of pouting. I'd hear Lucile
walk past the stairs toward the kitchen in her busy
self-important way. Maybe she'd leave. From a back
window of the sewing room, I'd see her in her car and
starting out the driveway. These were the least
obstructed windows in the house. Late in the day,
haze showed its tired agreement with the house next door,
the shingles dull and olive like the rusted screens, the
asphalt paper on the roof. I could see my aunt's
back yard on Chester. Trees as far west of us as Lake
marked off the streets in staggered elevations—palms,
short rows of deodars and jacarandas. At night,
from a window in the southern wall, the top three
letters on the tower for the ACADEMY kept coming on
one at a time, then all together.

 Before I moved there, while Dwight still had a
bedroom to himself, the upstairs hall had opened to
a sleeping porch. We closed the hall with a partition,

made a second smaller room that gave us closets and a
place for desks. It was the only access to the porch,
and I could leave that way by getting to the roof and
dropping from its lowest corner to the lawn.
But the roof had better uses. From its apex, I could
lift myself another level to the eave above the porch
where there were windows to the attic. I'd take one off
and crawl inside along the boards toward the open
hatch in the bathroom ceiling. No one would hear me.
Or back outside the attic, from the eave,
I'd use the beam-end as a hoist and pull myself
over the rafter to the highest roof. It had
good footing, a broad low pitch and several vents.
I don't know why I'd go there—maybe for the sublime
assurance that I could. Being there was almost to be
doing something. The sky went on at that one level,
intervened below the trees and rooflines and withdrew.
There was more to see than I could choose from,
the tallest buildings, like the Star-News and the City Hall,
too obvious to use as landmarks. I could climb back
down again with no clear sense of what I'd seen and go
collecting for the paper. People were home, and I'd be
nervous and abrupt, or sometimes pass the house for
others where there might not be an answer. I'd
fantasize about a friend of Polly's or the girl
somebody's brother fucked two times before her father
caught them at it and apologized and went away.
Sex was as foreign to me as a sense of how to
talk to people. I'd been born into a neighborhood of
older couples, widows, three or four small families
with teen-age sons or daughters whom I'd tried to know.
Florence thought they were too old for me.
My dealings with them were as strange as that one time
behind the Coles' with Jan and Helen when he told me
privately to touch her here. I hadn't understood

and botched it, made her angry at me, knew a little
better what he'd meant when he was giving her a
long and proper feel-up, which she seemed to like.
By now, I was as old as Jan had been. He'd seemed to
know what he was doing. I knew I didn't know,
and was convinced that my not knowing left me out.
The vagueness of the city when I looked at it
was my exclusion from the lives that made it clear.
People wanted it to look the way it did. The common
steady houses were their parts—lumber and stucco,
glass, the indeterminate and easy changes.
Streets were so well cared for and had so much shade
that they seemed more than what they were, or less,
another vaguer thing, the leisure, maybe, to be
somewhere else, a promise or perhaps a claim that
differences are good or never matter. I let it
keep what might have been its quality without me,
that "frightening calm" that Pasadena has for you,
its people there or not, inside their houses and in
no one place.

What did people do all day? I never asked that,
but I'd go downtown where there were people whom I
didn't have to talk to or to know. They were
shoppers and clerks and never seemed to catch me
watching myself in the parade of storefront windows.
I wasn't there for any reason. Every week or so
I'd go to a shop upstairs on Green and steal more
stamps from the show-books while I chose a few to buy.
She'd bring them to the counter—all the British
Colonies in the Americas: Antigua, Virgin Islands,
St. Kitts-Nevis, Montserrat. From the Bahamas,
a new series of eleven, clean, bicolored, all
consistently engraved. The 1/2d orange and slate-grey
Infant Welfare Clinic. Modern Dairying. And

Native Straw Work. Water Sports. A Fishing Fleet.
Out Island Settlement, with a bay and dock and
warehouses at odd angles, some of their roofs
the color of the paper, like the sky, the others
close consecutive dark lines. Each stamp had the same
embossed and perfect border. The Queen looked
pleased, but not at what the stamp was showing us
and not at us.

Scott's Catalogue and Album were at home,
and I still have them both, the stamps in their places in
flat tubes of cellophane, each checked against its
mint or canceled value in the catalogue. I've
counted them, 612, a third from Canada, the rest
from twenty-two crown colonies in the Atlantic or the
Caribbean. These islands were anachronistic
baggage of the slave and sugar trade, geographies of
simple dockets, bills of lading, ports, and putting in.
The manufacturers had wanted more. They drank to
"Markets! Markets!" at their dinners, and for
Christmas 1898, Joe Chamberlain had given them
a penny postage and a stamp that said "WE HOLD A
VASTER EMPIRE THAN HAS BEEN." They hadn't learned
that properties and goods were not enough,
that the sum of what they held was still a sum of
limits—land and factories and ships and
things that needed places: calicoes, bright shirts,
Stoke potteries and Sheffield knives. Even their
revenues were less than time, less than the
pure investment that the Germans made in knowing
everything—the languages of all their clients,
tastes, the smallest and most incidental changes in
production and the tariffs. Unlike Great Britain,
Germany and the United States were planners. Each
consolidated all its worries, tried to organize
the clutter of the unpredictable to make it

go their way. What went wrong in either war was
personality—bad planning what went wrong between.
Von Kármán's tunnel at Cal Tech could simulate the
turbulence a wing would meet in flight. It told him
which designs had possibilities and futures.
Growth was the provision of the time it took to
know that what was planned was right because it
earned more time to plan. Because the "Gibson Girl"
was heavy, bulky, had a kite-antenna and a crank,
an Army-Navy "E" Production Pennant went to
Hoffman Radio who planned and made a two-way
voice and code transceiver, which was small.
Their corporation flourished when the war was over.
They kept some military contracts, hired more engineers
who narrowed every unit of their work on TV
kinescopes and circuits. The beams of cathode-ray
electrons through a vacuum tube would synchronize each
thirtieth of a second. Successively, in league,
they looked like something. So that if you'd
wanted to, you might have seen what looked like
water, a level vaguely like the air between
the hybrids of white lilies. Seen bamboo, the
culvert where the pond filled. A slope with
ferns in the wet hollows, shade, the pouched winged
irises in their black pools under the trees.
Rough grass between some steps, the seedlings rooting
deep into the bank along the cool backs of the stones.
There was sun here, and poplars beyond the high
clipped hedges and the wall. You couldn't see the
teahouse or the smooth flagged path that had been
washed down carefully, fine residues of soil
still drying at the borders. There wasn't any wind.
From the street, the door of a garage pulled
up and back and a light went on inside,
reflected from the clean paint of the driveway.

A man in a white tuxedo left his house.
Someone smelled gardenias as she found her mailbox
locked with a lock she hadn't put there, its numbers
filed away illegibly, impossible to trace.
The son of a man I worked for died of a
bubble in his blood-stream. As a messenger,
one week near Sixth and Main, he'd seen a man
on fire and heard a window-washer scream and fall
ten stories to the sidewalk. When he went home,
his aunt was dead in the bathtub. He made the
phone-call, ate some cheese, began to walk around
unlike himself and asking quietly "Is everyone
all right? Is everyone all right?"

With my conception, I was virtually
coincident with cancer in my mother's body.
To exist is to be *placed outside,* where there are
things to fear. My body. Me. The visible
pulse at my right ankle, thick blue vein, the skin,
sunlight on my ankle in a cold house, now.
When I'm afraid, I try to think of everything.
I try to change the possible by thinking some one
part of it and giving it a place—gratuitous
murder, accident, a flood, the separate and bizarre
pathologies that could be mine and final.
Worry is somewhat less possessive, less complete,
more frequent and deliberate, self-amused. It too
displaces where I am with something that I make
inside me. Each thing I worry is secure,
familiar, almost home. Its difference is
mine and not the world's. The house wren, when it sings, says
"Here I am." It looks around and says it.
My worrying and fear are notices that I don't
have a place outside and don't know how to
find or make one. They are as free of people as a

garden is, or as a plan.

When my father died five years ago, Lucile
sold the house on Holliston and went to live with
Polly for a while. I was glad she was moving.
Pasadena would be less a place I'd go to
see someone I knew, be more the way I
wanted it to be—continuous, immune, with
incidental people. I'd spend the hour it takes
to drive there, park the car and walk up
Holliston and past the Nehers'. Theirs was
one of the houses that would plant itself
inside me when I'd read *The Life of Constable,* and
Roughing It, and *Madame Bovary.* Into the books that
pointed with interest to a certain place,
one of those places that I felt I knew would
intervene—not clearly, nor for any longer than
my time in walking past it. I wouldn't try to
keep it out or learn what it was doing there. I'd
commandeered it as a simple place, and what went
on inside it was as safe and constant as the
book itself. And since it wasn't just the Nehers',
since there were other houses too, what I was
after wasn't any single house but was instead the
possibility of houses, the abstruse sum of all
possible houses in that city, all of them
mine and filled with incidental people whom I
covered with my version of the Yahweh: I WHO AM
AM, and so the rest of you can be.

I know that it's otherwise—myself and other
unimagined people, their lives and mine, yours.
You had your own life there without my having
worried or imagined it, your difference
outside me, like the places that I know but more
surprising, more like those places that are
much more yours than mine. Like the Arroyo,

Mayfield, or Pacific Oaks. Like Bellevue Dr.
and Euclid, and St. Andrews—as far toward the
north and east in Pasadena as there were
houses that I didn't know. There'd be the streets that
neither of us thought about. Those that we had
were quiet and homogenous with now and then a
grocery store, a park, each street familiar but
indefinite within the strict geography of the
Arroyo, and the mountain, and those clear
aristocratic boundaries to the east and south.
In our stuntedness with people, what they
wanted for themselves resisted any little that we
made of it. What people did all day was
work of different kinds. On Altadena Dr.,
near Cooley, Roma Mulvihill consulted with her
botanist about the tree-ferns and the epiphytes,
a cool thick air inside her greenhouse as the
girls were dusting bronzes in the shop.
Scripps College was presented with the Charles Yale
Memorial Collection of fine presses, first editions,
and his specialties: The West, and Californiana.
At Aerojet, Fritz Zwicky thought about his
template of the stars for Project Rosy Glow.
Friends of my father's went on Tuesday Morning
Breakfast Tours of houses up for sale. Another friend,
"Rex" Rucklos, kept on looking for the men who needed
money and knew how to use it. H. Leslie Hoffman's
Easy-Vision Lens gave sharper contrasts. While he
arranged a point of sale or worked a coup for
college football, wrestling, and a recent film,
his tubes were mounted in blond cabinets and shipped.
Lyman Stewart's grandson was Executive Vice
President of Union Oil. J. T. McGucken had been
Papal Chamberlain, Domestic Prelate, and was now
Most Reverend Bishop, Vicar General of the Diocese.

Russ Peak, who made a fly-rod for the President.
The owners and employees of The Glass House,
Lytle's Roofing, Brotherton's, Crown City
Mattresses and Infants Socks. Clerks under the
diamond skylights at J. Herbert Hall's. Deliverymen
with the harried confidence to park their trucks in
anybody's driveway. People were home and working.
Harlo Mills, my piano teacher. Florence. Mrs. Shade.
You were home, your sense of what you knew extending
less as a line of places than as mornings
oddly alike and anywhere. And you were busy.
You were another person doing chores and things we
all do privately as what might happen to us
happens or doesn't.

      Richard Arkwright was a barber. He toured the
markets and the farms and bought the hair of
country girls and made it into wigs. When he
hired John Kay to build a frame for spinning
thread from the strands of cotton, manufacture was
domestic—looms and jennies in the kitchens of the
small freeholders and the farmers who would
sell their cloth to merchants. Wool was the English
staple trade, a privilege of the landed graziers.
All gentlemen wore silk. Raw cotton was a coarse
adherent fiber from Brazil and the Antilles.
It had to be opened and cleaned and have its strands
laid parallel by two large cards that worked it
back and forth between them. Drawing made the slivers
equal in thickness by redoubling them, and roving
made them thicker still and left them ready to be spun.
Arkwright's water-frame replaced the hand's inexpert
pulling and pushing, movements that begin and end
and can't repeat themselves exactly. At Cromford,
with the money of two hosiers, he built a gas-lit

mill above the Derwent. He needed journeymen
clockmakers who did tooth and pinion, a smith who
forged and filed. Afraid that no one man would know
"all that I should expect he might," he was
"determined to let no person see the works." He wanted
"locks and hangings for the windows; good latches
for the outer doors, and for the inner doors as well."
To make the other money come to him,
he specified as little as he could in all his
patents. And as he sold the plans, he built six
factories in Lancashire. At Glasgow, he was made
an honorary burgess and was taken to the
Falls of Clyde, at New Lanark, where he would
build another mill. He advertised for weavers,
framework-knitters. Children who were seven could have
constant employment. In the riot against machines,
they burned his mill near Chorley. He was threatened:
"I will lie in wait for you in this town Nottingham
or wherever I most likely to find you. I will
ashure shute you as your name is what it is.
Dam you do you think the town must be ruled by such a
barber as you." Contemporaries thought he was
a Newton or Napoleon. He was knighted and named
High Sheriff of Derbyshire. He claimed that
he could pay the national debt if he were
left alone to make his money; and when he died,
the income from his mills was more than that of most
German principalities. He was asthmatic. An
economist of time, he worked at English grammar as he
traveled in a post-chaise with four horses driven
always at top speed.
	He lost his patents at a trial in 1785.
The industry was open. In the damp valleys,
at breaks in the long profiles of the streams,
new spinning mills went up. They were too far

outside the towns to worry that they'd be
inspected—close enough to send their thread
to upland workshops by the new trans-Pennine
turnpike roads, or by the new canal that crossed the
valley of the Calder, through the Craven drumlins
east to the other watershed, and Leeds.
There was so much thread that barns were fitted up with
handlooms that could weave good fustians and cambrics.
Cotton was its own new country, and the landlords
feared the moneyed men. Land could itself be
capital, the business of the aristocracy.
Each landlord had his broken straggling plots,
their furrows running lengthwise to the rounded
headlands where the plough would turn. He knew
which land was his, but it was open and was grazed
collectively by several owners. Between
harvest and sowing, even his farmers' pigs would
graze there with the sheep. Cows grazed the catchwork
meadows on the terraces, or at the watersides.
Enclosure was the landlords' plan to change their
strips of arable to larger straighter fields.
They would appropriate the wastes—the marshes and moors,
the peat-bogs where the farmers got their fuel.
Commons had been "a profit which a man hath in the
land of another, as to pasture beasts thereon,
cut wood, catch fish, hunt coneys, and the like."
In most of the Midland parishes, there were now
Acts for Enclosure of the Open and Common Fields,
new roads with wide grass verges to a ditch,
then quickset hedgerows, ash, occasional small
farmsteads with a croft, no lanes, the landlord's
manor and his park, and in the fields the
thickets for his foxes. It cost him less to
graze than till. The stiff clay soils would hold
a year of wheat, another of spring corn, lie fallow.

The land would yield him more if he could save
the labor of his farmers and the cottagers.
Tenure at Will was his prerogative to put them
off the land when he was through with them.
As he engrossed more farms, they set his hedges,
drained and marled the looser tracts and planted
clover, turnips, and lucerne. He managed
breeds of stock and turned them out to graze the even
turf across the hillocks. Enclosure had made
"fat beasts, and lean poor people." With no one skill
peculiar to themselves, they left the villages for
workshops in the north. The Earl of Leicester said
"I look around and see no other house than mine.
I am like the ogre in the tale, and have eaten up
all my neighbors."

    Although you couldn't have because of other luck,
if you'd come in from Stockport through the fields
south of the Medlock, you'd have passed the first few
villas and their lamp-lit oval drives, your father
looking for a brickcroft and a kiln where you could sleep.
How much we'd know about you now would turn upon
how far you'd come. Your name could mean that you'd
crossed over in a packet-boat from Cork for the
summer harvests, hay, then peas, then onion-pulling,
working north with other navvies as the crops
ripened or were taken by the frost. Near the Potteries,
more tramways with their loads of coke, more furnaces,
white tips and slag-heaps at the edges of the fields.
There were fewer of you, and then just your family.
You'd found a recess in a viaduct, some driftwood,
scraps, but no soup-kitchen. Tomorrow night, you'd
be here on the outskirts in the kiln and thinking
God knows what about the possibilities for
any of you, warmth, or health, whatever other
standard things we might suppose that you'd have liked,

a peep-show caravan, or suet puddings.
Little Ireland was across the Medlock on the Oxford Road,
and you were all up early. For as long as you had
jobs to find, the streets would keep you looking
further into what was there beyond the frontages.
Through the entrance to a foundry, you could see the
dockside—cranes, a horse-dray, narrow boats,
the water out of your view below the worn stone
curbing of the wharves. The back-to-backs, doors
open to the floor inside: a chimney and staircase,
the bed a heap of straw with quilts of old sacking.
A woman told your father he and Wick could try
"that warehouse. The mills in Ancoats for the
lady and the girls." If you'd been taken on there,
we'd have lost you to the city as you'd found it,
Jersey Street, The Phoenix Works, long rows of looms with
straps from a central shaft, the oil, steam, the
operatives and overlookers, a flour-and-water
paste between your fingers as you dressed the warp.
We'd have lost how you were different from what you'd
done to stay alive. And as you'd stayed alive,
you would have been the things you'd known, things that we can't
recover, that we tend instead to think of
as examples of a tyranny, bad luck. We know that
courtyards from the narrow alleys were as
hard to find as they were rotten and undrained,
dark, with offal-heaps, small pens for pigs, a doorless
privy where the modest brought their feces in a shoe.
We know that there were eight or ten to every
room off these courts. Doors were their ventilation and
stayed open to the passages where everything lay
quietly where it was thrown. People were living in the seams—
in undercrofts of bridges and along the
rivers and canals where they would bathe, the water
warm from the boiler-tailings, dyes, and bleaches,

from the refuse that would lift through floors
of houserows slipping toward the Irwell and the Irk.
Crosses on the Ordnance Maps of 1850 mark the streets
where five or more had died of typhus. Workers ate
only the tainted meats. Their foodstuffs were
adulterated: flour, with chalk or gypsum; pounded
nutshells in the pepper, sloe-leaves in the tea.
Mothers were back at work the same day they delivered,
milk dripping from their shirts. Each wet nurse
had a dozen babies. She'd give them Quietness—
a dose of treacle, sugar, and crude opium—
and they would look much older than they were.
They'd go to work as menders in the mills. After their shifts,
too tired or too accustomed to the heat,
they'd sometimes hide away in drying-rooms and
sleep there and be roused and, still asleep,
start going through the movements of their trade.
Andrew Ure had seen them at the looms. He'd found it
"delightful to observe the nimbleness with which they
pieced the broken ends in that few seconds'
exercise of their tiny fingers." Habit had given them
"a pleasing dexterity." They were "lively elves
whose work resembled sport." It didn't look that way to
Engels. Children were in the mills because the jobs took
"cursory attention." Skills made a worker more
intractable and less dependent. As long as there were
"workers enough, and not all so insane as to prefer
dying to living," their master had it as he wanted it.
He had the capital to shield himself against
uncertainties within the market. And when those came,
the workers were displaced and worked for less and were
"as much without volition as the rivers."
Nor was the family a place for them. Children took their
parents' jobs. A family would last as long as
any of it members needed it for his or her own

interests. One family was all those people who might
unionize and ask their master what he meant to
do with them. His was another family. It was as
different from theirs as any printer of
bright shirtings was from his blue-handed boys.
Each class became a family by its distinctness
not from the other, which it had as well,
but by the differences its people might have
known where they had lived. Each family was
pure in the way that anything is pure when it is
distant from another thing that might have touched it.
If your family had suffered purely, you were
nowhere, like the figures in a photograph that's been
retouched to rid it of the blurs they'd left
because they'd been too close or hadn't posed.
If there'd been just that single difference between
yourselves and the bourgeois, you wouldn't have been out
below the gaslamps on Blackfriars Bridge and seen
the plane of brickwork past Victoria that held
exactly to the river as it came toward you.
The tall mill-chimneys would have been so much the
unexampled symbols of your lot that you would
not have looked at them nor heard your clogs along
the gritstone paving as you crossed in front of
Renshaw's to the geese and elbowed past the men with
billy pots and mufflers, women in their shawls.
Clerks who were hopeful of a partnership were
not there with you if their difference from you
was that one simple difference. No one was
with you in that crowd if what it meant to
be there was one's solvency or lack of it,
those categorical reliefs from what was there
around you to be known. People were there and in the way.
If there hadn't been those differences that
place us where we are, you would have been no more

in Fennel Street or Rochdale Road among the stalls
than in a garden with the Gregs or Cunliffe-Listers.
Those who'd made their landed marriages were
interested in your condition. Everyone was
interested in your condition, some of them
afraid that you would have enough of it and turn it
back on them. They envied you your "profligate
remorseless and unteachable behavior." And they
lost how you were different among yourselves.
You concealed from one another what you didn't have
and color-stoned your doorsteps as your properties.
"Anyone who did not own a hat would fold himself
a low square paper cap," but you were cruel to
dwarfs and cripples as the Methodists were cruel to you.
You hated sheenies, socialists, and any who were
"getting on." You'd found your ways to classify
within that undermass the simplest differences,
and what that let you miss kept you alive.
Since it was dense and fractured, raw, too small,
your masters left you to the world you'd made for them.
Their way out of the ignorable was to find other
places in the empire—St. Lucia, Trinidad, Lahore.
England had outgrown the continent of Europe.
Free Trade was Jesus Christ. They formed their
joint-stock companies and combines and could count on
triple rows of sheds, eight miles of granite docks,
calm and deep water in all tides at Liverpool.
They were still in that plain geography of
"things in their places," of bales on
hoisting-pulleys and in ship-holds and, along the quays,
the dry white scudding that they lost as waste.
They were looking for those samenesses that make us feel we've
broken through to something, through those
unsure things that happen in a place in time to
something like our safe impalpable and self-sustaining

plans that are always future. With the rhythms of storage,
their great facades in Portland Street had alternating
arched or pedimented windows, glass-roofed wells where
buyers chose their cottons in an even light and then
went on to the Exchange by Parker Street and George
to Market through the uniform four-storied rows of
offices and shops that lined the thoroughfares and hid
the workers' quarters and the inland ports and passed below
The London & North-Western trunk lines out of
Ardwick Station south at easy gradients across
five bridges to the fields.

     Suppose we'd want to memorize the present.
We'd begin with a scenario and follow it
toward ourselves from some one point that's both
beyond us and contained within our past. By
this time, it would say, our stock of capital is
constant. The Secretariat does not coerce. Instead,
it monitors and guides toward their optimum
the populations and economies of all the disparate
subnational and local interests. Behind its
sure administration lies the aggregate of what we
know and go on learning. We'd known we needed
families for all the different things we learned,
and so we'd organized them on some trees, in two
dimensions, like the trees that show our lineage with
names for leaves, with room enough between the cousins
so that all of them might marry and be fruitful.
Somewhere, casually, we'd found a branch that was an
axis, a manifold of what we could imagine if we
changed the metaphor and made it deeper, used
more of what was there and empty, filled it
evenly with boxes, drawers, a drawer for every
class of possibility and Possibility
itself a drawer, and Cost, Location, Schedule,

Shape, Who Makes It, How It Moves—as many
drawers for any plan as there were matrices
within each drawer for each particular that held
discretely to itself within its matrix, then
aligned or didn't as we made our runs to find
the one least suspect way to bring it off.
This paradigm was Zwicky's. He applied it to his
telescopes to know what driving gears he'd need, what
vacuum pumps. To know within what fraction of a
wavelength of light his lenses should be polished.
Which cameras and spectrographs. Which of the
photoelectronic fields that pull each impulse
through to a magnet that resolves, refocuses, and
sharpens it. The proper domes and mountings, screens.
Which engineers would build him the most stable
groundwork for the whole affair, with lateral
steel bracing as they use in dams. And where to
put it. Palomar. Mt. Wilson. Places where the
night sky glow from spectral lines and bands was
minimal, and where the winds in upper strata wouldn't
blur what he could see of supernovae bursting
outward toward quiescent faint blue stars. He
knew that's what they'd do. If he were thorough,
anything would do within its randomness what he could
plan that it would do. It helped if one knew how to
simulate a world, the way von Kármán did.
His tunnel was a closed system. It had its
own supply of air and kept returning it in one
uninterrupted flow across the surfaces of
streamlined wings and cowlings. In that thin
layer of air around them, he had found imaginary
drains and faucets that would change the flow and
shock their plane to spasms. He'd found the
Vortex Street, the drag on slender bodies like
the trout that Sir George Cayley watched in 1840 in a

pool below some shallows. Sand and fuller's earth had
shifted along the bottom, settled. With its
nose against the current, in its hold, the trout was a
spindle with diminishing resistance toward the tail.
Von Kármán often climbed inside his tunnel.
He'd lie out flat. He'd feel the way the flow would
touch him if he were the trout, "a well-fed fish of
thirteen ounces" and a length that Cayley had
divided into thirds and measured for their mean
diameters. Von Kármán knew that these diameters were
basic. They were the girths at common points along the
profile of a new design. The Bell X-1 conformed almost
exactly. And the Flying Wing. Rockets were something
else again. He leased an office from a former
Vita-juice dispenser, Henry Gibbel. He took in
Zwicky as his partner. He called the corporation
Aerojet and worked on tracking, staging, and the two
propellants that had blasted through a Cal Tech wall.
He'd had to move his people when that happened—
Frank Malina, Hsue-shen Tsien, John Parsons, Amo Smith.
He'd set them up where JPL is now, in the low
dry hills behind the Devil's Gate impoundment and the
spillway to the channel draining south beyond
the Vista del Arroyo where the nurses walked with
burned skin-grafted veterans of World War II.
He'd helped to plan the arsenals of Germany, Japan and
China, Russia, the United States. He always came back
home to Pasadena, to his sister Pipö and the
house he'd bought when he'd been lured away from
Aachen in the twenties. His lab off San Pasqual looked
residential and benign among the dorms with
courtyards, cool arcades, the same pale stucco as the
whitewashed or adobe walls of mansions
south of California. In wedges of streets
west from the Huntington, the luxury of deeper lots was

trees, those full tall stands of them on slopes
behind the houses and the arbors with their loud
wisteria and peacocks, trees that from the street were
backdrops for the pantiled roofs, for changing
attitudes and depths from house to house with one house
east a bit and closer to the curb, the next
less forward, taller, with a drying lawn, more shade,
the house itself no deeper on its lot than
his on South Marengo where he entertained
Niels Bohr, where Einstein stayed when he was here,
and Fermi. Pasadena was a semiarid
garden of trees. From the higher ground of Raymond Hill
east and north, from that corner of the city
out into the blocks of smaller lots across the five
flat miles from Eaton Wash to the Arroyo,
trees were the earned release from industry and from
the hot and bright long afternoons. Below
Millard and Poppyfields and Chaney Trail, there had been
orchards mostly with an interspersed few streets of
modest bungalows for the retired Mid-Western
patrons of the cafeterias downtown. By private
rights-of-way and by electric motive power,
they'd take the Red Car from the cemetery to the
sheds below St. Andrews, transfer to the stop at
Mission and Fair Oaks and change again and pass
the Ostrich Farm and follow the Arroyo
down toward the river and across it to the
terminal at Sixth and Main. Clifton's was a short walk.
Its waterfalls and grottos and lanais were less
peculiar to them now. They'd wait in line for trays,
then choose their dishes, pay, and share a table
always with another couple, the talk among them
friendly but uncomforting, designed to show
too much that they weren't lonely here and didn't miss
the state societies, their picnics in suburban parks,

signs on the trees to help them find themselves, and
buttons, Hog and Hominy, A Jayhawk, Flicker Tail,
the roll-calls of the counties and a speech,
then singing all together at the last about a
"land with its sweet-scented plains." It didn't
matter that they loved the new, they sang, they'd
"not forget the old." The trains had brought so
many of them out to "do" the state that they'd been sold
themselves and one another. There were the tours to
studios and missions and the beaches and to
Alpine Tavern on the Mt. Lowe run. They'd seen
everything and more, and what it came to for them was
the building that was going on, a growth they could
explain by all those landmarks and the days. They'd bought
into it and moved and stayed and found they'd left more
changes than they'd known they had. Their sense of
where they lived depended strangely on their
fitness to change, as if they couldn't know
without those changes where they were or what they
wanted in their lives. Living here was too much what they'd
thought it would be. The sequences of perfect days were
unavoidably what they'd come for. They should be making
more of what was there and possible at any
hour in that clear air. With all those possibilities
aligned for them along the tracks and poles and wires,
they should be somewhere else since where they were was
old already with their being there. There was an oldness
too about the Echo Mountain Incline to Professor Lowe's
observatory, about his searchlight that was visible
100 miles at sea, about his zoo and the museum.
His line went on toward the crest on trusses,
concrete piers. He'd planned to build across a gorge
a swinging cable railway to a great hotel,
but when his notes came due he couldn't pay.
The route from Rubio to Crystal Springs became

another of the trips that Huntington could sell on his
"Day for a Dollar" trolleys, 6,000 daily runs
from Redlands through the citrus groves to San
Fernando, out to Venice and to Orange over enough
wide-gauge track between the stops to reach
Nebraska or Hidalgo del Parral. The rails were
older than the growth that was the only solvent
business in the place. If those dispersed connected
cities didn't grow, there wasn't anything but
piped-in water, rails, electric power. It had to
grow by filling in. It couldn't do that on the old
fixed lines alone but needed rents and markets,
interests, more ways to make the land less simply
there and waiting to be bought. When it was bought
again, for more, at little down, good terms,
it brought its benefits to everyone from
that large trust that this was where to live.
The plans for roads could speak of trains with some
nostalgia. They had done so much. There would be fewer
grade crossings, fewer delays for trains because fewer trains,
more Chevrolets and Fords. Cars would take people
anywhere. At their own times and by themselves,
at greater intervals according to their speeds,
more people drove each day across the new
divisions of the ranchos on the secondary
highways, local streets, the points each car would pass
no newer for that difference. The empty lots were
old with impossibility. They were sometimes
salted with a pile of sand or bricks to look more
promising to buyers. The land itself didn't
go anywhere. Places were old. The things that
filled them had been planned and paid for, the profits
counted already, reinvested, spent, passed by.
Bungalows were less in fashion than the spanishy
flat shuttered fronts, wrought-iron bars and spears

and balconies with canvas awnings, doors with the ornate
churrigueresques that public buildings had and
movie houses, filling stations, churches, and the stores.
This was their Colonial Revival. It was
old in what it missed, that native aristocracy of
landed dons. Its counterpart ten years before had been the
Greene & Greenes whose oil- and soap-rich clients wanted
liberal free-standing houses that disclaimed the
sources of their wealth. The Greenes, like Morris, wanted
well-made things for everyone and wanted everyone to
make them, if they could. Cal Tech was still
Throop Polytechnic. It taught both sexes
carpentry and turning, architectural design.
The students learned to sew and weave and worked with
leather, clay, and metals. George Ellery Hale would
change that. From the Greenes' own patrons he had won
endowments for his telescope and for the funds it took
to bring more science to the school. He could foresee
pure research and technology as complementary
twin halves. The region was cut off. It needed
fuel and water, power. Geologists and engineers would
pay for one another's futures, for the futures too of
climatology and astrophysics. The future was
successive and successful answers to those
questions it made sense to ask. How far from the
earth itself could we project? And what was light?
In the calculus of variations, what was the mean
process of behavior in a species, in a
social class? Could we compute a place for
each of us within the equalizing
sameness of plan? If we overlooked nothing,
no single difference of temperament or will,
if it were all accounted for and stored and if we
watched it periodically and found it yielded
more and newer orders, it would teach us how to

master what was probable and make it pure,
assign it a completeness like the past's. It would be
pain alone that held its place, that couldn't be
planned away from that one body that was living it in
hope, not waiting, not afraid to know it wasn't
worth it, all that pain. It was worth it. There were
people who made it worth it, and the world. A cat came
sleepily from a thick shrub and stopped and shook it head.
There was time between the bleatings of the horn to be
reminded and forget again the huckster and his fish
two streets away, then one, then out of hearing, gone,
the shadows of the fences less alert as the heat gave
way a little and the peas were shucked, all changes
watched for now as if one were confined and sitting up
in bed, alone, with nothing but the afternoon
outside along the ground toward the lilac and the
cactus in the foothills. The room didn't have that
loneliness of rooms she'd stopped to notice in her
haste to get her gloves or hat, rooms where she'd
asked herself how lonely it would be to have to
stay there for the afternoon and not go out.
She was reading about North Borneo, about a
concentration camp, the Japanese, their curious
honor and the cruelty that came from it. She hadn't
seen that in them, doubted it. She wondered what the
spareness of the things they'd lived with meant to
sailors on the carriers. The glare outside was
just what they would have stared through for their Zeros.
From the promenade, on each crossing, late,
later than this, she'd watched the clouds curve up in
tumbles that had brought no wind. Alone, it had been like
seeing a place for someone else whom one might never
tell about it, filled, as one was, with the colored
presence of what was there, with how it all spread
back and away and rounded, shone, went dim.

It filled one with the ease of trusting that the
other person too was in a place. Nor was it lonely
here. Her chair. The dressing table. Desk.
A blue slip cast ware and a single tile.
Light from beyond the hedges through the mica
panels in the shade, the lamp arresting it,
steadying for that last rush of sun that left her wanting
nothing more, not the lamp itself for reading nor the
food her mother brought, fresh vegetables and custard.
Elva, She was Elva. Under the one twilight,
the Esterbrooks' on Allen, Helen Thayer's, the tiny
cottage of the Kelsos' in the trees behind the
Elk's Club. Las Lunas, the McGowans'. Peg and Herb
Cheeseborough. The Hezleps. Orville. Allie Lou.
There were others who were more like family—Lucile,
Florence and Glen. Jimmie was at Lucile's.
Jim would be driving home from downtown past
Elysian Park and through the tunnels, past the glazed
deep pocket of the reservoir he might not see.
It was dim already in her bungalow at school,
the pasteboards in their slots, the sheets of rough
construction paper sorted by their shades and sizes.
Both rooms smelled like sweeping-compound, glues,
like the stark poster-paints in jars with white lids.
Occasionally, a car would turn from Madre onto Del Mar,
behind it and ahead along the streets
the separate conversations in the houses, trysts,
an evening with the radio. The sky was a pale wash.
It caught outside the windows all the late
small matters on the lawns, and lights inside were coming on
too soon.

    No sleep for either of us on the flight to
Maine and then to Gatwick. From the train, back yard
allotments and cooperatives, the city hardly

there at all outside Victoria and there inside it
only as a crowd. It's hot, of course, and everyone
just manages. We pass them in their queues. They need
maps and bookings, taxis, other trains. I try to think they
like some part of this. It would help me through the raw
worry of what to do if I could think they
liked it in some way I didn't. I ask about the
Grosvenor, and it's silly to have asked because it's
here, inside the station. We take our bags upstairs,
come down again, go out to look for dinner, eat,
come back and go to sleep. When I hear it, I know
first that it's coming from below, from that odd warm
hollow where the people were and where they must be now,
still purposeful and hearing differently this voice.
A woman's, young, it names in series all the single
destinations, platforms, times, then carries here with
nothing that disturbs me, nothing I can understand,
no word, with nothing lost, no listening and only
letting go, forgetting.

    It's rarely that easy. The ease of it has
little to do with how tired I am. If it's before
midnight, if there's still time enough to sleep,
I go to sleep. At two or three, when I wake up,
I have to be asleep again within an hour.
I shouldn't let it bother me. Even if I
don't go back to sleep, I shouldn't worry that I haven't
slept enough, that I'll feel it in my eyes. If my
tongue won't work, if it makes me slur the things I
press myself to say, I'll say just that much less.
I should ignore all day in what I do each
thought of myself and how I'm feeling tired.
I work at my breathing for a while, listen to
Linda's and adopt it, a sleeper's breathing.
Mine would be slower. To breathe the way she breathes,

I'd have to be awake, and am, have been awake
too long now and have given up on trying to know
exactly what I should be doing, how I could be
thinking about it all and changing. So I don't
care if I go back to sleep. Since it never works to
care about it, since my calmness when I care is
feigned and crazy, I don't care. I'll get up.
I'm too tired to get up, I'll give up here. And even the
giving up is trying, a counterfeit that takes me into
harmless things, a seagull, my socks, into the drowse of
someone giving up who meets that first improbable
ellipsis, slips beyond it to a second and a third and,
losing count, goes off between the scatter, sleeps,
is someone who's asleep, not me at all, who's only
almost there and pleased to be this close, too pleased,
now coming to my hold again with all the shifts
intact and unrelieved. I've lost my chance.
Having been so close and missed, I can't start over.
Nor can I trust that even now I've given up.
I'm left remembering the times I've gone to sleep,
and what I've done each time is to forget.
It's happened before. I've slept. I was asleep an
hour ago when nothing woke me, when I was simply
awake. I didn't have to see that it was still
too dark. To know I wasn't where I'd been
two nights ago, or one, Les Bouilladoires, Cassis,
I didn't have to hear inside my head the
syllables of Juan-les-pins. It might be different if
once for any fraction of that irreversible one
moment I could be unsure. If I had to sort through
where I was and was it time, if there were
sequence or change, some need to tell myself I'd
done it again—that for another night, and here,
again, impossibly, I'd placed myself too soon—
then I'd have doubted, sleep would have given me

doubt, resisted me a little, made me wait,
kept me for just that long from knowing that it's
me who brings this on and can't undo it, who won't
live it as it is, as mine. The certainty that
sleep isn't there is me. At angles, in
parentheses and stacks, my waking pulls me on
from this to that and this and I can't
stop them or go back or choose, they're all the
same to me, I make them all the same by
hating them for keeping me awake. Each part is my
excuse to be sure. It lets me prove that there are
others like itself, that I can be replacing it with
others, each itself replacing what I want until I'm
sure that I won't have it, sure that wanting sleep is
helplessly safe. Since sleep is all I want, there's
nothing else that I'm removed from. Wanting is a bore.
I can distract myself, contrive a lustful graphic
time of it and feel it take, my penis, by degrees,
my proof that things can change. It's more like
doing something to get up and walk. The bathroom door,
the light. Although I've taken it too many times, my
doing this can be a start. I spill them in my palm.
Fourteen. They're grainy and pale, a uniform
clear score across each face. This one. When it works,
it's like a tiredness I take inside me. It
weakens and breaks, dissolves inside me in a
gradual prolonged slow carry into sleep.
It isn't tiredness. I'd have it to go
back to if it were. I'd trust it as a need.
I'd do what willing sleep won't let me do,
I'd rest between my tiredness and sleep and
wait for them to take me. I'd feel them
measure, as I came away, my heading toward.
Repeatably, on either side of sleep, there'd be a
time that I could wait for. Going either way, I'd

wait and be pleased. It would be time to be
awake now, time to sleep, my tired surmises
tired of themselves and me and, given up,
forgotten in my rest. It's my remembering that
tires me when I'm doing badly, doing what I'd
willed I wouldn't do again—the same embarrassing
explosion over nothing much, self-pity, fear.
I've willed too often that I wouldn't be afraid,
that I would quit my way of thinking
backward from a safer time, the symptom or the threat
behind me then, the drive and its risk survived.
My going somewhere wouldn't be my getting
past it in time, past it to my staid, more certain
memory of how it was, of how my wanting
not to be afraid had tired me, made it hard to
start at any time with what was left. I miss the
steadiness I sometimes have that lets me
stop and go back, begin to choose, defer to
patience and surprise and incompleteness, loss, to
versions of things, the sense we follow when we're
talking to a friend and knowing that he
understands us, wants to tell us too a
story that he wouldn't tell if we'd been
with him all the time. There isn't time for stories,
there's too much. My friends aren't here, and I'm
forgetting what I meant to ask or tell them
yesterday, the day before. And when it
matters that I try to keep it, when I
prop it with its mattering and call it up
again, another time, I feel it isn't
theirs anymore, it's mine, and it's too dear, I
keep it with the others that I've blurred and kept,
the dead ridiculous and grand collection all I
know about my time. I write to someone,
you, I say I like it here. I say that I'm confused.

I know these rifts and these delays are still
forgivably ahead, that I can start.
The differences we don't catch up with aren't the
incubus I make them be by wanting
always, all the time, a hold I don't
forgive myself for wanting. So I want something else.
I want my balance to be alternately
there and not, the way it is when I'm up
walking somewhere and forget my weight—
around me, and in balance, in the world,
the things I'll never think about or see.

He says he's Antony, no "h," they've spelled it
wrong on the card he shows me, someone in this
hospital has spelled it wrong. It's Thursday. He says
tomorrow they will tell him when it's time.
He'll start to fold his clothes and put them in his
suitcase—first the pants he isn't wearing, then
his underpants and socks. He'll wear a different shirt. So
this one that he's wearing now, he'll fold it too—
this sleeve across, this other one. He'll put it in his
suitcase, on the top, his shirts are last. He'll pull the
zippers all the way until it's closed and then he'll
lift it by its handles, carry it across the rug. The
door will be there, he'll open it. He'll go on through the
hallway to the door and open it and come inside toward that
other door. He'll go on through it to the
anteroom, the door and steps, the car. He'll put his
suitcase on the seat behind his mother, close the door.
He'll get inside the car, in front, he'll close the door.
I want to let him tell me all of it. I want to
wait to hear the things he'll do and let it
please me that he'll do them. And he will. He will be
back here, after Sunday, every week, and every
Friday he'll go home. But I'm not listening, I'm

ahead of him or still behind, he's in his
bedroom with his clothes unpacked and then he's
folding them to come back here, he's Antony, his
name-card again, it's Thursday, then his clothes, and I
excuse myself. He says good-by as if he knows he's
told me enough, I could have stayed but he's not
sorry that I'm going. Or I've made that up. Because it
sticks for him and won't go on without his
thinking what he'll do, I want him to be
used to something. Even if it's being left, if
that's what he's used to, or the place. Another
visitor who listens and then leaves is
habit for him, he's been left again, he has to
start with that each time or give up being
used to being heard. A lady's saying
hello to him now, he's telling her his name.
Rehearsing what he wants to feel he's up to
helps him, makes it all right. It's all right,
it's not too much for him, these Fridays. Almost
beyond him, in the car, his mother asks him is he tired,
would he like a nice cream gateau after lunch.
She knows it's hard for him to listen. He can't be
ready enough to hear what someone says, it can't
belong to him, it shifts, keeps coming in and
tires him with its wanting to be heard.
Beyond him, almost easily, the traffic and the stops,
the roundabouts for Market Drayton, rain, the M.
Her trouble at the exit is too far away,
too close, he can't align it, doesn't try, it isn't
here, inside him, like his knowing he should wait,
she hasn't told him yet. They're still not there,
and now they are, she's told him, he should start.
He's on his feet outside the car. The door doesn't
catch at first, and then it does, and each
disturbance through the last unfolded pants is

very near, it's next, it's here, he meets it as the
wave of deeper places that he can't make fit.
She's switched his dresser and his bed and it's all right.
Behind this change, the little more that he might
look at, sometime, from his room. His curtains lean
abruptly onto nothing—light, the day, the different points,
whatever he excludes that otherwise would
stop him forever as its dumb too thorough
index of how much there is. If it's fine, he'll go out
into it on Sunday. His father doesn't
mention any more that they're out walking through the
Brynlow wood. They see the butcher and they
keep right on, hello, and yes it's lovely, yes he did,
did he? At the escarpment, when they wait,
he doesn't know his father sees some farms,
the Pennines to the right, and Stockport, Hyde, the Greater
Manchester conurbation, its line below the moors
less generalized than how it looks on mid-scale
insets in the Irish Sea. The world is plural
only as it shows what each of us sees differently.
Inside its different aspects it's the same.
We try to get inside what lies between
the ways it looks to us and how it is.
We want to know it. Maps are a way
of bringing into sympathy and our control
all levelings and projections on its curved replete
outside. We sink the benchmarks, measure
sides to another benchmark. We take our
stereoscopic pairs of pictures from the air and
scan them for a true relief. When we've composed
one scale from which the others all derive,
we print in stages with the different plates
these lines and colors, these details. The map for drivers
simplifies the contour. It supposes that
obliquely, from the northwest corner,

sunlight in its wedge is giving us a bleached
readable surface. The single sheet has
Scotland on the other side. In three languages,
the legend to the left explains that there are
primary destinations. These have been marked.
Between them, with their distances, an interlaced
blue for the motorways with green and red.
The numbers of the routes don't interrupt the
junctions or the names of towns. Slopes that face
away from the light are shaded in a freehand grey that's
heaviest along a ridge. There are spot-heights. We can
see that the Norfolk Broads are flat, and the fens,
that the clays and chalks all differ from the
uplands somehow. To hint at any more than that would
darken it. Places we'd be driving would recede,
their script too timid. The series of seventeen
Quarter-inch sheets is solid color—light green and
yellows for the lower ground, then buffs. Among
other codes in the margin, a totem helps us know how
high we are if we're on crosshatched beige.
It's a busier map. The rails are black, there's black
stippling for the cities. Its overlay of roads is
blue again, and red, and brown. It shows us the lanes,
the narrow tracks with passing places. Steep grades are
arrows with their tips downhill. We'd use a much
larger scale to walk by, larger than the old red-covered
Inch-to-a-mile, and brighter, with no hill-shading, only
outlines of relief on a blank ground, and fewer
meddlesome details. We'd carry the sheet
with us as a prod to keep us looking for the
footpaths that it says are there. If we'd left the car
just off the A-road and had done all right,
if the trace along a wall had led us clearly to
another in another field, and so on, and it was
fresh there, damp at our feet and drying in the wind,

we might be starting to forget it wasn't ours.
The gates that ask us please to close them, latches that work,
a huge horse-chestnut in the line of hedge across to
that slight rise, the barn there, rooks, "all the fine
cattle going about that would do your heart
good to see"—it isn't ours or any Cheshire
dairy-farmer's. It's the map's, a pure informed
plotting of the rights-of-way through features we can
bear on when it all goes wrong. Where the path's been
lost to a tractor that had ploughed close up, or where
the hay's been cut, where we're left with only stubble,
when we see, beyond the windrows, at the copse,
a stile or a gate and cross toward it and it's
neither, just the fence, and more of it, around us, here,
there's still the way we came. From the disused
railway that we passed, or from the hill, we'll line up
Bexton and the Toft Hall spire. We've overlooked a whole
miscellany of clues. It makes us want the next
larger scale again, and the next, their narrowing
systems of intelligence on how the ground arranges
outcrop and cliffs, loose boulders, intergraded
trees over coppice over scrub. The river's been
moved a little to the right so we can read the
mean high water and the low, the pumping stations,
weirs and sluices. Roads at this scale are still assigned
conventional widths. Only when we've started
in from the country, when the path in the grass verge is
sidewalk and it's mapped, when the treads of the
steps are mapped, and the curbs, and we can follow
house by house the numbers or the names, Japonica,
Pendennis, Lucknow, Manor Dene—only at twenty-five
inches to the mile are the strips that take us places
truer to plan. We measure ourselves, we know how
broad we are at the hips or shoulders and we're
there on the map, provisionally, in scale.

We see exactly what allowances we'd have to
either side if we were centered, if there were few enough
people on the streets that we could center ourselves
exactly. It's what we try to do outside the
Royal Exchange, or on the ramp to an upper
story of a car-park. In adjacent sheets, the map
shows us these things to scale. Each permanent
feature on the ground is shown to scale until, at
1:1250, it's easier to list what *isn't* there:
tombstones and vaults; small sheds in private gardens;
signal-posts in the neighborhood of a large
marshaling yard, like Ardwick; repetitive things—
letter boxes, transmission lines on single poles,
bollards and capstans on the Salford quay.
We're shown in plan the thickness of an outer wall,
its juts and its recesses, where it thins.
If they're five square meters or more, we see, from the top,
all courtyards, light or ventilation shafts,
each well in the Portland St. storerooms crossed with the
symbol for a glass-house roof. We don't really see
inside. Even at this largest scale, we're shown
nothing in the way of rooms. We know from the
Bureau of the Censuses that rooms are surely
countable and counted, that people are themselves
accounted for, by survey, with their clear consent,
in confidence. All subjects are assured that they've been
chosen at random, they're a sampling, maybe it's
where they live, or their job, the interviewer isn't
sure, really. May she come inside? She needs their
age and sex, are they married, what type of a
household is it, how many people here are
catered for at least five nights each week by the
same person? Are they employed? At what? Would they
look at this chart and say within which group their net
income is likely to fall? How much and what kind of

education have they had? Is this a detached or
semidetached or terraced house, a flat? And how many
rooms are there? There might be questions too about
amenities and cars and contraceptives, episodes of
physical and mental illness, deaths. They're asked for their
opinions, sometimes, and are probed. Could they explain more
fully? In what way? Some answers are foreseen and we
precode them. Or we close the terms. "Here are
six sorts of behavior. Which would you disapprove of
most in a married man, a friend of yours, who is
not in the police?" We frame the things they say. When they're
compatibly and cleanly numbered, we can run them through.
To any number we can always add one
because it works that way, by adding numbers.
Because it's small, because our maps for it are much
larger than its surface, we've learned to print in
silicon, on chips, an integrated plane of
microchannels, spurs and gates. Its circuitry will run
twelve thousand operations in an inch,
the bits, with their addresses, there, inside,
not going very far. Because it remembers
perfectly, because it never sleeps, because it can
sort and compare and choose and find the proper
order in the sum of all its pulses, ON or OFF,
the things they say in eighteen million homes are
digitized and stored, revised, called up again by
GEOCODE with its coordinates for any point
P on the map, all references on grid and bearing
east and north in equal squares from their false origin.
We're somewhere in its mesh of cells and always
catching up. There's always, just ahead of us, a
rate or table, an estimate of trends that we
belong to and that waits. We watch it as we watch ourselves,
expectantly, afraid that in the calculus of
pain and pleasure, at the scale of 1:1, we're not

happy enough. To be happy, we have to be sure.
We'd be surer if enough of us were happy.
This many will kill themselves, this many won't,
or we'll be off a little in our reckoning.
As predicates of what's been well-rehearsed,
we're either well- or ill-behaved. To help us know
the different points of stress at different times, we're
averaged out, depicted from the top with all our
furnishings—and there are scripts. The stir at breakfast.
Sandwiches are being cut. We see how much room
Mother needs at the work-top when someone else
passes behind her with a tray. The toddler wanders
in and out of the kitchen as she tidies up. She's
bathing him now, lifting him from the tub: is the floor
wide enough here for her to towel him dry?
We need our clearances and kinds of peace from
sideboards and chairs, settees, rectangular or round
coffee tables. They steady us, these things we've made.
We move between them, retrieve a sameness from the same
bookcase, the same clock. People don't always want to
watch TV when it's on. They need a place to sit
away from it so they can talk or read. And in the
bedroom? Should they try it with more pillows?
Standing up? What is it that might singularly
please them there as they imagine it being
better than the last time, than the best?
Is it how she'd seem to know before he asked,
or that her breathing as she came would take him too?
In the quantum of their parts and how they move,
where are they when they've started? His cock's
inside her and they've started, her labia
just visible around him on the outward strokes.
It troubles us that we don't quite see to the
heart of a place. Whatever shows itself
conceals its other sides and how it works.

She's leaning on her hands, astride him, her face
strained and turned away as, in and out, more
surely now, he feels her start to ease beyond this
time they're keeping. He tries to slow her but she's
past it, past her wanting. And as she comes,
it's like the wakefulness she leaves when he's been
holding her and waiting and her shudder tells him
now, now she's asleep, she's left him, and he comes.
Equal, complete, their bodies are as far away as
outer is from inner, then from now. As if for
each of them inside their separate minds
there was another who was listening to them think,
they're not so much alone as by themselves.
They're thinking. Neither speaks. Infinity being a
funny number, we lose them to themselves as each
remembers and awaits, concurrently, from
anywhere in time and nowhere yet, another
part of what they're thinking or a pause.

    We've rented this house for seven years.
I keep thinking of the back yard as something I could
know but don't have time to, it would take too long, I'm too
busy at school, or here, or we're away, I
postpone it, save it for a time when I'll have more
peace with my nerves. When I'm doing the dishes,
I look out at it and remember some of the names,
eugenia at the kitchen window, flagstones,
St. Augustine. There's a jasmine border with three
squat confused palm-trees, oleander, a sundial,
a cement squirrel. Since it's something I can
do there, I like to mow the tiny matted lawn.
The bathroom the Brainerds added on in 1964
pinches and shades the clothesline. We cut the holly
back from it, and the pittosporum too. And on the
longer days, in May, before we leave, the sheets are

dry in an hour. If I were simply to
watch them for that time, if I watched a bottom
corner of one sheet and waited while it kept
bending and going slack, I'd be hearing
Coast Highway, tires in a lane, a truck, more cars,
too many for me to tell which way any
one of them was coming. I can sometimes tell at night.
If I've heard it for a while before it's here,
it's from the left. Place Realty mutes it.
So do the trees in the ravine. Coming from the
other side, it's past Cabrero's fence before I
hear it at all. I listen to it go away.
Another from the right, a few more. And then none.
A gap between them always sounds much longer than it
ought to be. It makes me strain to hear
through it to the next car. Or maybe I'm thinking
backward to the last ones, wanting to hear them
south now in front of the trailer park, and north, in town.
It's late enough that the roads seem less like the
same one road. A certain interchange—like each
wide flat bridge across the next dry river, it's
almost a place. Or the Canyon. Driving it now with their
brights on, they watch the shrubs for lights of
cars coming the other way. They feel their dimmers
click when they press them, click as their brights come
on again when they've passed. The drivers didn't
see anything of one another's faces.
What do we see of people from our cars?
Ahead of me on a road through small farms,
two couples who've stopped to talk. They walk to the side.
Looking back at them in the mirror, I can tell I've
broken up their meeting. It's early and very cold,
and I can see the words between them as they leave.
Where a tractor had turned out onto the road,
an arc of dried muc. My tires throw it

up against the undercarriage and there's
snow in the furrows between the new shoots,
on the corrugated roof of a shed, its gutters
dripping a little. I was seeing what was easier.
A farmhouse, pollarded trees, the rest of it,
it was easier than seeing people. At the far edge,
beyond the fields, the tall flared top of another
water-castle. People were going on
forgettably with what they did, but not right there.
The postman was there in his yellow truck. He had his
route to do, I knew that much about him.
Housewives were in the shops on their various
errands and charges and were coming back
out into the cold. An hour or so before,
I'd seen them in the square, in Mirepoix. They were
all I'd had to go on. Waiting in the car, I'd watched
this one or that as she shifted what she carried,
took the step to the arcade and disappeared.
I'd noticed a Citroën, how its steering
kneels to the side it's turned to when it's parked.
Then Linda, with our lunch, and we'd been on our
way again by the map on another day of seeing
just what we wanted to, whatever we could,
vineyards still, and farms, a walled city, I was letting
signs and the names of places as they came
withdraw to the place which then itself withdrew,
the next one to the next as seamlessly as if
none of it were missing. Except when I was
with them on the streets, it wasn't like people, like those
junctures with them when I think they might be
looking at me too. To someone who lived there,
what was I doing in Morbegno? How long would I stay?
Coming back through town each day to our one room.
Winter, a mountain to the south, noon. The sun was
glory for that hour we had it and I walked on

into it, its channel between the fronts
three stories deep. In the glare from bricks laid
vertically in swirls on the steep street, people were the
sounds they made. A woman. We passed. Even in her haste
she may have seen my strangeness. I couldn't tell.
It would have been all right for her to look,
I couldn't have seen her looking. It's usually
not all right. We shouldn't stare. In cities
our mix is random. We glut the streets with intricate
crossed-glances at things, a news-rack, a display.
If we belong there, we don't want people to
see that we see their faces. Sometimes they do.
Is something wrong? they seem to ask us when we're caught.
We cover it up. For as long as we can, we hide.
And what do they want who look at us? They want what
we want—sex, or talk, whatever's missing,
whatever we look to fill. We can't always know.
What the derelict want is usually too clear.
They halloo us with their eyes and we're ashamed,
we pay them so they won't keep looking. They
eat the shame and drink it, they survive, they stay
shameful for us, they show us that our needs are
shameful, that we agree to that, that even they agree.
We see them crying to themselves on benches in the sun.
They walk the gutters. Alone and talking loudly,
screening their mouths with their hands so we won't hear,
they step to the sidewalk, accost someone
ahead of us on the sidewalk, whom we pass, listening,
wanting to hear what they say. We should give up our
places, they say, they've given up theirs.
The person they've stopped tries to keep his place.
I tried to keep mine with a lady in Fulham Road.
She was saying "Can you help me, are you
important enough to help me? You look important,
will you marry me?" She said we'd share. She was a

seer now, she saw through stories to the All-at-once.
Where I was born, and when, how I look, who my
friends are, what it falls to me to do—she could see
through all that to a deeper luck that was
hers and mine together while I heard. She wanted her
place back, could I help her, it was my luck too.
I wanted to show her that it wasn't. If she didn't
disgust me, there'd be little that we shared, I'd be
protecting her, she wouldn't have to see how helplessly
timid I was and self-estranged. I couldn't talk.
I was afraid to be disgusted. She could see.
Our hearts were there. Neither of us could hide.
And we were married by the awe that lay between.
I got away from her. I walked. The different streets
joined and went on obliquely and I followed them,
I didn't try to read them for their hearts.
Where should I go? Inside my template for the
stations and the parks and squares, I was getting my
place back. I'd gotten away from her, had to, even with
Linda sometimes I have to turn away from looks that go
on like that commandingly. With friends too. How long should I
hold your look or you mine? It's a time that's too certain,
that leaves too little room for the tacit
losses and trusts that are the time we live
away from our friends. Alone, we have to stay
used to ourselves so they'll know us. Have they changed?
We think what they're likely to be doing now,
with whom, and where. We think about their hearts.
Are we too important to them? Not enough?
Would they assure us that they're glad we're who we are?
I travel very badly after a while. Morning
and midday and evening and meals and
finding meals, finding a place to stay—
those are the junctures. I feel I'm what I

might have seen but didn't. Or what I might have found to
say about it all if there'd been time.
My longing for it now encloses it in my not
being there to let it get away. From here,
from this house we won't come back to after June,
I take my time remembering a walk.
Corners, a city block, the names, the typical
street-furniture and traffic. I could have
stopped outside the windows of the shops,
prolonged it, stayed alert, kept trying to absorb its
ordinary hidden business. Like the rest of them,
I'd gone on. We were all of us in the
middle of something. At her leisure,
looking at clothes, a girl with a bag, her other hand
behind her at the waist and holding lightly her
right elbow. People waiting to cross. With their first steps,
they were that much closer to my losing them.
To a question that I tried to overhear,
a woman answered at my back that, no, she didn't
think of herself as being bored. And the man who stretched
forward at the curb to see around me. Was he late?
What he was called to was another day,
to that one part of it I might have learned by asking.
Along the boulevards, in 1840, the *flâneur*
chatted with whom he pleased as casually as the
pace his turtle set him. I try to imagine him
subtler than that. Although he'd talk with them sometimes,
they'd rarely place him by the way he dressed
or by his preference for districts. Letting the crowd
inscribe him with its hurry and its looks,
he'd be its marker, watching—it would be by
him that we might figure who we are.
Disdainful, and preoccupied, and tired,
it's what we miss that makes us passers-by.

I meet someone. We talk. We're both a little
surprised that it's that easy. Am I sounding
too cordial, too relieved? It isn't
traveling that makes me ask, I do the same thing here.
I think too much beyond my part in what I'm saying.
Is this other person interested? I can't be sure.
To shame me out of wanting to be sure,
you've told me that you think I'd feel more
interesting if I were dying. That just might
do it, you think. It might remind me more that
I'm interested, me. I wouldn't lean so far
ahead of myself, I wouldn't have to,
I'd have my closure with me as I talked.
Maybe it's what I want. I hope you're wrong.
I still might ask you "Have I told you this before?"
We tell each other things that are only
starting to make sense. If they seem to make
more as we tell them, and if we go on,
what is it that we're leaving out? We're past it now.
Whatever it was, we didn't have to say it, didn't
break with it in the way that talking breaks
open, within it, between its parts, a time for
other parts, intrusions, more chances to be
missing what we meant to say. Linda was
awake one night and wanted to tell me where she'd
gone with them that afternoon. They'd parked at a
power station, where it was flat. There were tracks
already for their skis and they skied there until
Giorgio or Pironda thought they should go around
behind the village by some poplars and try it up
that way. The buildings thinned out and there were
sheds with animals with piles of straw outside and
men in some of the sheds and outside too with more
straw for the animals and bringing out the dung.
She had to go around bushes and small trees. She kept

falling, and they all laughed and decided to come
back through the village because it might be easier.
The street was ice and hardly wide enough for
two of them at a time, or for a cart.
They felt showy in their bright nylon.
A woman with a bowl looked at them from her door.
Chickens. A covered water-trough. She told me
more about the street and then remembered.
What she was saying, she said, was that there were
farmers out working in the snow.

The Lover's Familiar (1974)

Matins

This hour is for the lakes,
for their patience as they look through themselves,

for the light they see there,
the splinters of light
falling over their sunken ledges,
and for the patience of those ledges,

for the trees they listen for and never hear,
for the rocks,

for the cold that knows the lakes
and comes to them
and covers their clear eyes
and calms them.

Lauds

For several blocks to any
side of the schools,

sheets in the hallways
of the small houses

are laundered and stacked.
From their drawers

they send guttering
and tiny points of fire

over ivory and china,
the porcelain

basins and white tile.
Radios on the nightstands

sleep fitfully,
their dials translucent

windows to a fever.
Moths tunnel in the lawns.

A palm tree waves and waves.
At the curbs, the streetlamps

are unharried. Their hum
steadies to the hour.

They are everywhere
with their vague languor

as across the city
the span of each beam

rests against the next.
The shops downtown wait

absently for their Dark Night,
their glass fronts filled

with baubles and odd
trappings of their fall.

All shelves are arranged
in boredoms of clean trade.

Milk leaks a spare light
evenly through its aisle.

Below the scales in
steel bins, the almonds lie

paler than ever, sleek moons
swallowed by their own shells.

The Very Rich Hours

Amant in bed,
dreaming.
There are no
borders to this
miniature.

B moves Bateau across the night.
It is all the loops can do
to let their gilding
bulge with what is there.
One light on the wide sea.
The bones of stars.

No other country is so
curiously watered.
From the estuaries to the very
sources of its inwardtending channels,
it rises in fogs which are themselves
arterial. For its earth
has more than once been seen
quite early in the morning
to lighten and give way.

At the gate to the garden,
Fair Welcome.
She raises her hand.

Salutare:
to greet and to save.

      Leisures of tendrils are on all sides,
      winding with the snails
      through white acanthus and discarded
      badges of pilgrims.
      You may assign to the nineteen
      portholes in these borders
      whatever you like.

The sand is of such fineness
and the flow so singly clear
that nothing seems to pass through,
golden, and with all its lights.

      Water makes very much the best
      portable horizon.
      While its reflections are
      fainter than those in the speculum,
      their angles may be measured
      accurately
      and the differences from a true meridian
      reckoned by the clock.
      These sightings should be taken at least
      three hours
      before and after noon.

Two liveried falconers,
the jesses and bells, the gloves.
Amant with the dove's neck-ring,
The lady in her chamber.
Winter trees, rooks in the white
branches, hounds, the dying boar.

On the top of a mountain
a lion waving his tail.

    The general course of the river
    straightens, and is moderately timbered.
    Scattered islands covered w/willow.
    Across from a single, long bluff of open rock,
    the plain to the S. is higher, extending
    quite to the mountains which contain still
    great quantities of snow.
    A small creek falls in from this side.
    Pursued its bottom for perhaps 4 m.
    Cottonwood. Much evidence of beaver.

Now all of this is to be understood
in a spiritual manner.
Let us cover
the nakedness of our fathers
with the cloak of a
favorable interpretation.

    Under a dry stalk of burdock, iron-brown
    latches and fittings, a few nails.
    The bulls are eating apples.
    Thick grasses sweat through the whole pasture.

Dame Reason with her
chaplet of apothegms.
He should put his heart
in a single place only.
The truest things about bodies
are their shadows.

    Pleas put me back
    in the water I am

Paddle-to-the-Sea

She has done this before.
She wades into the current
to the one point where the current
lounges at her hips.
She stands there.
With all the time in the world,
steadily, she kneels steadily
deeper, to her shoulders, smiling, her hair
cupped in both hands behind her neck.

      The Familiar gives Its first
      lesson to the lover.
      A new order
      is one that is renewed
      hourly.

A drove of geese in its tall, while file
plucks home through the wet fallow.
Hedges darken between the fields.
Along the wolds for miles in level tracts,
haze from the lime-kilns.
All quarters of the sky are wintry, huge.

      We could no longer be sure
      that we had passed the Préveranges.
      Freshets from the little stream
      poured onto the lane, filling
      ruts and drainages. In the dusk,
      and with our shoes soaked, we set
      off through a meadow, and another,
      and found soon an abandoned
      cottage of some old forester.
      We determined that I should

stay and secure it as an outpost.
Meaulnes went on alone.

At an earlier hour,
the ground at the wood's edge
illumines to some thousand
footcandles, fades under the
canopies, the layers
of trees, of shrubs and herbs,
under the dark itself,
brighter by as many
eyes as are buried there.

    Tied to a washboard,
    submerged,
    the panes of glass
    chime like clean ice.

they are dangers harebells and
just where the fall goes over
they lean into the spray so
far and bob so on their stems
they thrill and a hammer rings
carillon down the cows spine
feel it there it goes again

    Death hath its seat
    close to the entrance of delight.
        —Gudique

Sifting over porches and limp hibiscus,
rust from the canvas awnings,
its red spores dull in a moon that shows
everything, houses and driveways,
fishponds, all of them

hiding from their insides, forgetting,
looking around.

> there is no way to lie down
> and not lie in the same way
> that someone has had to lie
> thinking of how far it is
> to the places no one goes
> or to any place this far
> from the beds where the dying
> cry into the night this far

Deacons and presbyters.
The Laying On of Hands.
In a vial,
juice from the wild cucumber,
powdered glass,
the divine Endura.

Prime

Towers look across
to other
towers and to tall stores.
They look to the mountains
which are their help.

The sky comes down
weightlessly
into these
spaces the town leaves.

With the lonely
grace of what it fills
it comes down

weightlessly
and is all of it,

is the sky coming there.

Terce

Between the walls, the brim
between the air and the water
fits, presses where it can into

corners, into cracks that freeze.
With its pressing into their sighs
it spares the walls

nothing, sends them for breath
into their own pains,
into what they remember about being

one stone, breathing, the brim
away somewhere, not pressing.
As it slips through their dark course

the seams that once bound them
narrow and clutch, shudder to take
more, to take enough,

coming and coming to be so close.
The brim curls at its edges, lapping.
The air and the water go their ways.

Lutra, the Fisher

The otter is known
for the way his face turns up
anywhere.

On silver coins
or from behind mahogany bureaus

he wears the aspect of a suckling,
innocent
and helplessly

shocked that he should be caught so,

napkin under chin,
his dinner folded
head to tail between his jaws
like a limp bow.

When he goes to work

the surprise is
that he is there at all.

His long neck of a body
streams like sunken
weed-strands,

rises and trails the quiet wake
of any log or stone.

Even in the shallows

he is the thought of his own
absence
and can be found at home

as water would be found there,

filling the den
or strewing over the kitchen floor

bones and vermillion gills.

Itinerary

The farmhouses north of Driggs,
silos for miles along the road saying
BUTLER or SIOUX. The light saying
rain coming on, the wind not up yet,
animals waiting as the front hits
everything on the high flats, hailstones
bouncing like rabbits under the sage.
Nothing running off. Creeks clear.
The river itself a shallow, straight
shoot to the north, its rocks mossy,
slick above the few deep pockets.
On another drainage, the O-T-O.
Loose stands of aspen on the slopes.
Dude cabins, their porches and split-log
loveseats, dull yellow curtains
slapping over the open sills.
From Emigrant north to the Great Bend,
loaves of haystacks, stud farms, charolais,
steel flumes between the ditches.
Access to the river's acreage
closed to its whole length, the county roads
dusty, turning onto the high
shelves of side valleys. Scattered
shacks and corrals. An old homestead,
the sod roof rotting out its timbers.
Below the spurs from the higher range,

basins in the mountain pastures
fill with odd water. The henbane dries.
Ruts cross in the grass at a schoolhouse.
Each runnel mixing where it can
the spring creeks deepen and go on
easily, swelling to the larger
tributary with its pools and banks.
At any bend the willows bend too,
and gravel bars on the other shore
flare into the shallows. An encampment.
Ponies wade to their knees and drink,
raising up now and then to look
out through the smoke to the near hills,
the one plateau heading off beyond
the Crazies and the Little Belts, north.
It strikes the river at the Gates,
the water piling through its broad course,
level, ridges and the vertical
faces of bluffs crowding to each side.
This rock is of an excellent grit for
whetstones, hard and sharp. There is here
more timber than below the falls. A spring
immensely clear and of a bluish cast
boils up near its center with such force
that its surface in that part is strangely
higher than the surrounding earth.
I heard today a noise resembling
the discharge of a piece of ordnance.
Unless it be the bursting of the
rich mines of silver in these mountains,
I am at a loss to account for it.
As the passages about the falls are
narrow and steep, and as the buffalo
travel to the river in great herds,
the hinder part presses those in front

out of their depth to the strong current.
Their carcasses by the hundreds
litter the shore below the cataracts.
We have made of the mast of the pirogue
two axletrees. Walked ahead to my first
view of the falls, hearing them from afar.
Their spray is scarcely formed when
bodies of the same beaten water thrust
over and down, concealing every shape,
their whiteness alone visible.
We will leave at this place all heavy
baggage, the red pirogue, and whatever
provisions we can do without. Needing
a cellar for the caching of our stores
we set hands to digging. More white bear.
These fellows leave a formidable
impression in the mud or sand. Goodrich,
who is remarkably fond of fishing,
caught many trout of two different species.
Came to in a handsome timbered bottom
across from the entrance of a very
considerable river. Its character
is so precisely that of the one below
that the party with few exceptions
has pronounced it the Missouri.
The fork to the south is perfectly
transparent, runs rapidly with an even,
unriffled surface. Its bed is composed
of round, smooth stones like those of rivers
issuing from a mountainous country.
If this latter be the one we are to take
we should encounter within 50 miles
a series of precipitous falls.
There is now no timber on the hills.
The black rock has given place to a

yellow and brown or black clay, brown and
yellowish white sandstone and a hard, dark
freestone. It rises from the water
abruptly on both sides in varied walls.
I could discover above their horizon
only the most elevated points.
The river retains both its whitish color
and a proportion of its sediment,
but it is much clearer than below.
The banks afforded us good towing.
This method of ascending the river
is the safest and most expeditious.
We pass a great number of dry streambeds.
These plains being level and wholly
destitute of timber, the wind blows
violently with its loads of sand.
Driftwood comes down as the water rises.
The banks are falling in very fast
and I wonder that our pirogues are not
swallowed by them. Wild hyssop grows here.
A few cottonwood along the verges.
Undergrowths of rose and serviceberry,
and small-leafed willow on the sandbars.
Met this evening the famous white bear.
I had rather deal with several
indians than with this gentleman.
Much less ice running in the river.
We make ready to set out, the party
in general good health except for a few
venereal complaints. A windy,
blustering day. Our two pirogues still frozen.
I draw a connection of the country
from the information of traders.
The falls are about 800 miles west.
Rose early and commenced roofing

the two wings of huts. Our situation
sandy. Cottonwood and elm, some small ash.
We must now settle for the winter.
Very cold. Hard frosts. The river falling.
For several days we pass deserted
Mandan villages along both banks.
The beaver and otter are becoming more
abundant. We put ashore at noon,
setting fire to the prairies to signal
that we wish council with the natives.
These Arikara much reduced by pox.
It is customary for their nation
to show its grief by pain, some cutting off
two smaller fingers at the second joint.
The earth of the plains is in many places
opened in long crevices, its soil
indifferent and with a kind of timothy
branching like flax from its main stalk.
Delayed here today so as to take
equal altitudes, the weights of the
waters of the two rivers, their specific
gravities. As we near the great Platte,
the sandbars are more numerous, sawyers
worse than they were below. Mulberry,
oak and walnut. These prairies from the river
have very much the appearance of farms.
We continue to pole our way upstream.
Nothwithstanding our precautions, we
struck a bar and were near turning over.
The sergeants are directed each to keep
a journal of all passing occurrences
and such other descriptions of the country
as shall seem to them worthy of notice.
Our hunters report deer in every copse.
I got out and walked for one mile through a

rush bottom, nettles as high as my breast.
All the forepart of the day we were
arranging our company and taking on
those articles we will need. St. Charles.
The men spent their last night agreeably,
dancing with the French ladies, &c.
My ride was on a road finely shaded,
with now and then a good farm. The corn
in tassel, its leaves of a deep rich green
bending at the ends by their own weight.
Wheat and oat stubble. A hilly country.
I passed a toll-gate, and, looking back,
had my last view of the town's steeples.
From the state house cupola I could count
the buildings, the number of which was
ninety. A wooden bridge crosses the river
just below the town. Men were engaged in
racing their horses. I sought lodging
and was shown to bed in a large barrack
where a man and wife conversed with me
until I feigned sleep. This is a post town,
the mails arriving from both east and west
on Wednesdays and Saturdays. A young woman
gave me directions from an upstairs window.
I descended the hill into Frankfort.
There has lately been established a large
manufactory for spinning hemp and flax.
It is wrought by water and keeps in motion
1200 spindles. The streets of Lexington
cross at right angles, its stores filled both
with imports and with local goods: fine
cutlery, tin ware, muslins and nankeens.
I was so well put up that a man would be
fastidious to a fault to have found
the least thing wanting. Approaching the city

the land changed steadily for the better,
no longer broken, as to the eastward,
but fine extensive levels and slopes,
the road very wide, with grazing parks,
meadows, and every spot cultivated.
The farms hereabout have generally
good and spacious stone barns, a few acres
cleared but for those stumps or girdled trees
still standing. The neighbors found last year
a human jawbone, rough and honeycombed.
My wagoner arrived this afternoon
and went on, appointing to be in
Louisville before me. I pass a house
with small turrets at its corners, lawns,
the whole needing only vineyards for the look
of villas in Provence and Languedoc.
Noticed along the banks of the Holston
phlox with white flowers and phlox with pink flowers,
two different species, very small
phlox with lance-shaped leaves. Where I
come in from Abingdon, the Kentucky road
divides, the other fork for Burke courthouse.
With nothing to do I make ink from gall nuts.
More opossum taken in the woods.
This animal's greatest peculiarity
is the false belly of the female.
She can draw the slit so close that one must look
narrowly to find it if she be virgin.
The air clearing this morning, I was
surprised with a full prospect of mountains.
This river where we leave off is 240 miles
distant in a straight line from Currituck
Inlet. The turkey-cocks begin to gobble,
which is the language wherein they make love.
We have a dreamer of dreams among us

who warned me in the morning to take care
that I not fall into the creek.
I thanked him and used what caution I could,
but my horse made a false leap and laid me
down in the water at my full length.
The sky at sunset had a swept look.
There was risk of our dining with St. Anthony
when one indian knocked down a fat bear.
Of the stem of the silk-grass their women make
small aprons which they wear for decency.
They put these on with so much art
that their most negligent postures reveal
nothing to our curiosity.
The ruffles of some of our fellows
were a little discolored by the bloodroot
which these ladies use to improve their charms.
Bear, it would seem, is no diet for saints,
for it is apt to make them too rampant.
At night, the surveyors took advantage
of a clear sky. This trial of our variance
shows it still something less then 3 degrees,
so it remains much as we had found it
at the sea. We have now run the poles
beyond those inhabitants most inland.
There fell a sort of Scots mist all the way.
I have learned how rattlesnakes take a squirrel.
They ogle the poor beast till by force of charm
it falls down stupefied and senseless.
The snake approaches it and moistens first
one ear and then the other with his spittle,
making the head all slippery. When that is done
he draws this member into his mouth,
and after it, by casual degrees,
all the rest of the body. I am not so
rigid an observer of the Sabbath

as to allow of no journeys to be
taken upon it. Nor would I care,
like a certain New England magistrate,
to order a man to the whipping post
for daring to ride for a midwife on the
Lord's Day. And yet we found plainly
that travelling on the Sunday had not
thriven with us in the least. The rain
was enlivened with loud thunder, and there is
something in the woods that makes this sound
more awful, the violence of the lightning
more visible as the trees are shivered
quite to the root. This Great Dismal Swamp
is the source of five several rivers.
We run our line to its skirts, which begin with
dwarf reeds, moist uneven ground. The season
inclining us to aguish distempers,
we were suffered by the resident to
cut up wood for firing, drive away the damps.
At the bottom of the account Mankind
are great losers by the luxuries
of feather beds and warm apartments.
We perceive our appetites to mend,
and though we have to drink only what
Adam had in Paradise, that stream of life
runs cool and peaceably in our veins.
The days are hard. Our slumbers sweeten, and
if ever we dream of women they are kind.
I delight to see the banks of the Inlet
adorned with myrtle, yet it must be owned
that, sacred to Venus though it be, this plant
grows commonly in very dirty soil.
Norfolk has most the air of a town
of any in Virginia. There are now
riding at her wharves near 20 brigantines.

The trade hither is engrossed by those
saints of New England who every week
carry off a pretty deal of tobacco.
I have found that after my devotions
a walk in the garden can do much
to fill my heart with clear obedience.
I repair me there that I might think
deeply of the earth and how it will be
all too soon my sleeping-place. For I am told
to fear such things as bring me to ill terms,
told of those who seek congress with the earth
that they shall have her in their time forever.
That her places sing their love-songs for no man.
That I am not the suitor whose betrothed
awaits him, but some unwelcome third
with God alone her lover. And yet I would
look upon such country as will show me
nature undressed, the strata of the land,
her lays and beds and all her privacies.
For my wonder tells me I should be
promiscuous, should learn by all the
laws of bodies and by where they are
the joyful news out of the new found world.
This walk is news. Its bodies point me always
in and out along some newer course.
There have been divers days together
wherein alone I've watched these flowers
buoyed on their stems and holding up the sun.
Just now I catch them thinking on themselves,
composing from their dark places the least
passages for light, tendering how they look
and how I look on them. It comes to me
that the world is to the end of it
thinking on itself and how its parts
gather with one another for their time.

These are the light, and all the forms they show
are lords of inns wherein the soul takes rest.
If I could find it in myself to hide
the world within the world then there would be
no place to which I could remove it, save
that brightness wherein all things come to see.

Sext

The air binds in sockets
around its few trees,
their arms crazed and spiny.
Tailing from the loose floor
shines where the sky holds it.
For as far as it carries,

the Dead Heart takes its hour
deliberately, this full light
scraping through its washes
and over the tired outcrop,
missing nothing, rooting in all
fissures, wearing it down.

The Inland Lighthouse

Into the night,
out from him,
out into the air
he throws his frames
and fixes them,
holds them out there.

These are his shores.
The waters never
rush at him, never
follow the beams
back along the watch
to his lean shiver.

Around him, as he
turns, he hears
a dull tick of grains.
He stares into the day.
Sand fills the sky
with its falling

and he turns and turns.
'Nowhere. Nowhere.'
It is his oath.
He is the light,
the keeper.
He is not to leave.

Nones

The day has found next door another
roofline tiles next door again some shade
prim clotheslines furniture the chalky

stucco of garages haze and trellised
carports driveways gravels fills of brick
old angles down the inclines where the

grey and scored warm plates of sidewalk
level with the aprons there is more
somewhere than these streets their careful yards

The Great Garret, or 100 Wheels

The curricle and hansom
pretend to such size as would send them

shaking along the lanes
and past the gates to closes,

their separate pedigrees lettered
neatly on each undercarriage: 'H. R.

Waiting' and 'Thos. 1775 Beeton.'
They huddle among the rafters with

models of sedans, wains, herring carts,
cabriolets and a barouche,

all kept at rest in some autistic
pageant of transport, or by the staid

examples of the wind toy, its soldiers
frozen forever in mid-stride.

Only the cycles have a muscular past.
From the treadles of the *Draisienne*

it is as far to any point on the whole
vast chase of the manor

as to the next of the measured
interstices between the spokes.

Turning is what would change this.
Because they never turn,

the niceties of the garden are clearly
here, nearer the pediments than those

outlying, lesser strips of arable.
Clearly the forecourts are not behind.

Predictably, and with perfect rigor,
they front for the house in its fixed

severance from the village and the fields.
Because they never turn,

landmarks of this and that are where they are.
Wooded hollows and the Windrush.

Stray brakes of hawthorn on the slopes.
Sheepwalks. Trails. Uncertain rights of drift.

The Queen Anne Cottage

The paths are dutiful.
They swell up only as the contours
call upon them for help.

At slight rises
or where a tree has repressed too much

they are at ease.

Sometimes they cross one another
and go off toward so many enclosures that they startle

even the novelist.
They evade her like poachers
just as she is placing her mansion behind the firs.
She is left supposing they entered the garden
here or maybe
here

and the clouds cannot wait for her
and the dusk loses its memory and shines
and the old berlin draws up in front of the wrong gate.

Or they may pass as roads.

The horizon can seldom tell
if they are coming or going.

They make it turn itself out into the distance
again and again.

The Queen Anne knows
that this is what the paths have to do.
She likes their seriousness

how they address the steps
with no hesitation take them
boldly and steadily at perfect
angles onto her veranda floor.

She thinks they are the boards of this floor.
They have no trouble staying down.
The nails are not so much
holding them
as wanting their heads to find
a good level place.

If she is the paths
they do not come into her at each side
as she does not go out.

Everything turns so
on where she might be said to be.

If she is the paths
and trembles with a light fine
palsy through the whole
Valley of the Sweetest Name of Jesus of the Earthquakes

the dust that rises with the shaking
covers her secret flanks

tight draws
where foxes slant through yucca on steep
switchbacks to the crests.

If she coos to the hills to play
Touch Me Here
and
Honor Thy Creases

if she calls them her Dove her Supper

they quit their prayers
for steadfastness their

meditations on the ease of plains and on the
holiness of vast distresses of boredom they
breathe her as if their being
expires where she
leaves off.

If she is breathed
she is no longer in the delirium of seven
hardships the hardship of

triangulation the hardship of
Great Bandy Leg Walk the hardship of
construe the hardship of
summer sketching tours the hardship of
porte-cochère the hardship of
it is not permitted the hardship of
doctor doll with skull on its foot.

Her walls give over their absurd disguises
if she is where the paths stop.

Yes when they are called upon to lie down
as she herself feels called upon
to lie down

her walls give over their absurd disguises.
If she is where the paths stop

her gambrels and dormers and spindles
and ramped rails
give over their disguises and she is left with
everything she can see.

There is sweet alyssum for eyes.
Its flakes of petals are the presence of all color.
It is on its way out into the world.
The benches take it on they need it.
Without it the palms are forgotten and workaday.
The mud can wait forever but it goes there too.
At the reeds and bamboo flutes

it slides with the frogs into the pond.
It is amazed.

Here is the sky insisting adamant letting

nothing have its way nothing no not the
lilies trying to hold it off nor the carp coming
up through the tight blue
membrane no nor night nor that obscene fruit
the moon.

The sky is as secure within the pond's shores
as in the hollow of its own hand.

It tenders the Queen's profile.
Cupola.
Bracketed roofs
and thicktongued scrollsaws.
Baskets of fuchsia hanging from the eaves in
ponderous drooping scrota.
White straight chaste colonnades.

From the heart of the pond
the sky tells the simple happiness
of spilling over weirs
evenly
as with an eye to glass.

It tells of the blue
turrets of Azay-le-Rideau
rising like a surprise from intricate
watercourses.

It goes on and on
and tells that she herself is
the River Stour grazing through fields

flat

her eddies
whispering around stumps of old bridges
that she will not be back.

For below a single
hay wain crossing at the ford

below the mill

dense oaks are waiting to be spelled.

Their sequestering has brought them to this.
In their cells along both banks

the river is their solace from far places
their window

and as they draw from her

their higher branches
open with a faint gold to lower
clusters of oak

to the gold of the fields

the sky

to the dark rich
amplitude of the far clouds moving on.

Vespers

They were taking back
against themselves to their first springs
the evening and its light.
They could be sure of wells,
had lined those holes with the cool
liverworts of upland coverts.

Their readiness was in what they knew
of doorsteps and of worn stone bridges,
how they had drawn around them to the broader
millflats, slowing, the cattle bending
quietly to their own tongues.
There was the dry-dock baggage:

ladles and cauldrons, ribs,
new barges waiting on their timbers.
All shows of trees,
the open looks between them to the hills—
they would take these back and cleanse them,
they had been their widest there.

Its Time

Conserved in dews.
Yellows. The yellow

distillates of white.
How the heat in its

mean free path fills
inch by inch the blue

middle distance,
each plank and leaf

deeper by each plane,
each body saving

place in the late
morning. Squat barges

adrift along the
towpath. Beams of locks.

The canal, its calm
glazed heart bending

inland, further,
between the fields,

a seam in their deep
brightness, saving up.

How change is saved
in strong parities—

for the grasses, the
light of any hour,

grasses for what light
the clouds let through

over Homestalls,
Mithers and Trims' Green.

Stores of it in jars:
from the Common,

mosses and lichens,
barks, her colored soils,

the umber, pleated
furnaces of dank

mushrooms. Its true darks
lost under varnish

of violins,
of cart grease, tar

or snuff of candles.
That its time on all

surfaces is change;
that these accidents,

its meetings, redden
through interiors

in flares and rich
traces of its source;

that its colors and
colored lights and shades

withdraw around the
leaded mullions,

its low angles
framed against the walls,

changing, each canvas
sure of what it holds;

that it lasts this long
is light's strangeness.

Compline

Gudique is the chastening.
She is not a fish.

She is not the rocks where she browses
nor the pools.

The river when it opens
is not Gudique.

When its forgetfullness
falls from it,

when a cold wind leaks
upward through the drifts and folds and

pours over the banks
and over the ferns

this is not Gudique.
Gudique is the chastening,

the river forgetting
Gudique is the river.

New Poems (1996)

She

      The back of her neck.
Crazy to think she'd like your

hand there sometime.
It would never happen that from way

inside her or from long ago she'd will that it be
your hand there and moving, the fingers

only at first and just the tips,
no impress, no

leverage from the knuckles. Until she
wants you to, until she strains invisibly

outward from her wanting toward your hand, you can't
alter her neck's exposure to the air,

you have to leave
entire and maiden each conjectured place her

skin starts on the way inside.
Proper to her body are its

lineaments and heat, its chroma, what she
ate this morning. As you greet her you

do something with your eyes and mouth
that shows you want her in your

arms now. She lets you see that that's all
right with her, she's

for that, and then her
shoulders are there, her clothes, it isn't

sexual, of course, how
could it be since where would

trust go if it were? Trust is
here with you both, you

feel it in her body,
she trusts that you'll be letting

go of her soon so you can
each of you start talking, there's usually

news enough, and isn't talking
just what the doctor ordered, isn't it grand?

She listens and talks.
She's as much herself as ever. It turns you

outside in, you're her
convert,

it's required of you that you keep doing
better since she's here to watch.

You're doing worse. The more
riotously you crave her,

the duller what you find to say. This
fluff you're telling: it's the anemic puling

child she filled you up with and you bore. Take it
away from her now forever. Hammer its sorry

brains out. Strangle or starve it. Fix its clock.
Don't let it grow up wanting.

Pretty Blue Apron

0

In the separate histories
wanting writes,

zero doesn't count. Nothing had
happened yet. Zero.

Then it had. There was placental
discharge and infusion. These didn't

follow one another as the night the day,
there wasn't time. With nothing

private for it, undeprived,
the fetus took in everything as

one one one one one without one
"and" between,

without once knowing it was only one.
It got born alive and there one was,

1

a positive and whole number. Into
all one's chances, one unfolds

head first. God only knows the
start it gives one. One has toes.

Reaching for their lost water, each
wiggle of them squeezes through a one-way

pin-hole in time. It's too
much for one to tell that there's an

outside. The heart can't
swell any more toward it and

caves back in,
starts over into every ma-thump mortal

quaver it has left. For all one can
do about it, which is zero, one stays

2

proper to two. No two,
no one. There's second-person

fostering out there somewhere or one leaves.
Two could hardly

bear for one to have to go without.
Born to

see and be seen,
one sees two's face. Two

smiles as she nurses.
When the nipple slips away and isn't

there for awhile,
two's face is there. "There is" is

either of two's nipples, two's one face.
Between one's wanting and the two that gives,

there is a place for things to happen.
Is that look happening that one so wants?

To lack it takes up
one time: two looks, and it

arrives just at one's body at time two. All's
well again, until, again, pressed

forward so that now again, almost
before one lacks it, one's moved

out of the good. Where
is she, that good slaking mother? This one is

looking now again, that's better, good,
one's own smile shows in hers sent

back to one, and so on. After
long enough, there aren't

two mothers anymore, there's one whose
badness one says no to as one also says you

papa, you blue apron, you my lamb.

The World at Large

In whiteout, with its
incident reflected light and no horizon,
the ice-cap might be thought to pass for nothing.

There's nothing to be thought about the

0
nothing as such.
To think how it might

be with the nothing

1
gives it away already as something that is.
Already, as that nothing out of which
before one is born a whole
world of things might let one see them,

there'd been the nothing's manifest

2
jointure with ice.
For a thing to interrupt its having
not yet happened, it has to be

changed to itself by something other,

there can't be even
one without its alternate of

nothing at all. As it might
never have been,
the Greenland ice-cap was already

I

one thing to see.
Out of nothing on one
sketchbook-page, a Swedish artist
eaten by a bear had made show,

convex-upwards, a reserve that,
melting, would consume

most of the world's great cities.

Its mean daily temperature is
twenty-two below. Constrained by
rock walls, the radial

outlet glaciers at the end can only
fracture and shift.

Sheared off, they do their

likeness-making as they topple,
each surface sending out
displays of how it might be found to look. So

instant are they,
so much
quicker than the time they take to see,
that one's eyes

trained on them in series can't make out that they're not
still inside the bodies they had left. As simulacra

themselves are tribute,

tribute also when a membrane lets them through. Pressed
into,
all souls have organs that contract the spoils both
joyful and sad.

I

In a motor dory from the parent ship,
one could take the old Norwegian

wireless station for one's bearings.
Closing with it over the shallow bay, and
landing, walking toward it,

one could fix as one's new point

the lower right-hand corner of the right of the two
downstairs windows.

Once one was there, one could press one's
finger there and wait.
Everything else would go on as it was.
But even if one weren't only touching it,

even if one could

be that point so forward in the mitered trim that the next
closest point was air,
what a very strange

thing it is that at
any point along that coast there'd be an

on-plumb right angle. Against everything

else there is to see, and at
more points still,
the station is for now a tight
alliance of angles, its door on the back

upwind side.
Barrels are at hand in front, and
turf-stacks, poles.

Before it had these countermanding things,
Myggbukta was a few

poorly defined beach ridges,
the low flat foreland and the bayward slope.
There were calved bergs out past the skerries.

Up the hill, in summer, ribbons and fields of
ice were left. Holding it

open to be seen,

light scoured the next cross valley to its top for
day-long tiny changes.
It wasn't seen.
No person

kindled there
the fire that lets things show as

lakelets and
thin tundral cover.
That kept it one.

Over landfast sea-ice in the sounds and bays,

2

an Inuit cortex,
its million billion hook-ups rummaging for

depths and movement, angles, light.
From times before on sleds it sorts out
more or less remote and

upright faceted obstucting

ice-drifts, it grants the hunter
distances he needs from what's at
all times ahead. He needs to
tell on the run that one

after another he can dodge
ahead of him the chunks extending

up from the wished-for level course. Around each dog

ahead of him in harness are his
propositions. Telling that
two are about to foul their traces, he proposes that they

slow and reroute.
In the mid-day twilight, he might hear

shoreward from him at a point too far his own ice
moan at its moorings, shudder, heave and raft.
Ice has its customary
way with them all. The people are

steeped in the ice, the ice is both

outside to them and
in. Marked off inside their ice-walls is an air

calmed as they would calm
inside their bodies the disquiet that there's
nothing to eat. There are no caches of bagged

guillemots left, and on the drying-racks
no char.
It's good that seals make
breathing-holes in the ice. Sometimes they lift out

onto the ice through leads to open water.
For longer than a

day sometimes, stock-still, a hunter

waits in the future-perfect.
It needs to have happened very soon that
there at his feet will be

a seal he can sink his teeth in.
If he treats it well, if before he

flenses it with his knife he gives the seal a
drink of fresh water,
that seal will come
back again, it will give itself

again to that hunter in

many other seals.
As he eats the liver, he would have made it all
one for himself if he hadn't carried

with him over the ice in his first-person body
the charge from
other persons
not to let them die. Determinate

figures of them are abroad.
On his sled-run back, they ply
toward him in their hides and fur.

He tells them his luck.

Touching it with the soles of their boots,
villagers with

buckets and polyethelene bags
claim from the hunter their portions of the seal.
With as many of them on the ice as there is

food for,

they are that one
withdrawal from their disjoined bodies
of how the ice would look if they weren't there.
The lot of them might well have

starved by now. They might have
stopped having young. Though two

among them have conceived a third,

it could miscarry.
There are the bone-jamming trips by
sled each spring over the hummocks. There are

salmon to be speared, the women standing
thigh-deep at a river-mouth in spate.

When a baby is given

                    3
birth to,
the mother cuts the cord with a sliver of ice.
She finds the Mongolian blue spot and

licks the baby, wraps it in
rabbit-skins with the fur facing out.

                    4
Before they pay their
visits to one another on the shortest day,
the people rearrange their faces. They stuff
wool in their mouths,

they flatten their noses with string.
"Are you from the
north?" they're asked. "How did you get to

look like this? You must have

passed through the intestines of a dog."
For as long as they can, from

door to door, they stay
unrecognized, speaking in falsetto.
They scare the children. They are required to dance.

When their hosts are able to

name them again at last, they're offered
snack-cakes and coffee, cigarettes.
Taking their turns,
all come to call except

¹

the *qivittoq,*

the man who went into the mountains
disappointed in love and with
no prospects. Just because you don't

see the *qivittoq* doesn't mean he
doesn't see you. A year after his
kayak had been found
near The Place Where One Capsizes,

4

he was heard by some to stifle a
cough one night outside the windowed

back wall of the church.
From the northernmost
ice-free port as the days lengthen,

the ferry calls irregularly with

mail in its holds, and
software, and seal stew. The harbor
busies again.
Since with Home Rule subsidies for fishing,

the halibut and tom cod in the fjords are
"money in the water,"

prow up
outboard-fitted skiffs pass the submerged
blue edges of the floes.
Presenting its whaling tools and Norse lintel,

the museum opens at
noon each day under the green and yellow

Explorers' Club flag.

The solstice arrives.
A grave is dug with the pneumatic drill.
The new Danes on contract to Panarctic Oil
keep to themselves as, on the small frame

storage huts and workshop and most houses,
paint comes in for much good use.
There are the summer packet-boats

south to a connecting
Grønlandsfly shuttle, and from the runway

up, it's all
icefloes and rock, water, a luscious
paper-marbling,

Greenland from the air, that much of it
manifold in the oval frame of one's
eyebrows, nose and cheeks.
Because it's

I

one thing only to itself and
stays one,

as soon as
that much of it is out of
view again,
there's more. There's

more than enough one isn't.
It affords things to see.
In remembering,

in hungers and estrangement,

in too often lacking
grace in the forms one seeks, in

relays to the
brain's neurons that were
surface tissue once,

2

one breaks things up.

If one didn't always have to do that.
If one's insomniac night-watchman could ever be at
one with the world at large.

To be any

1

bit down there in its ice-swoon, to seize

thoroughly, as all bits do,
the nearest, largest others. Nearest for

one bit of air, compressed, that has to rise, are
bits that compress it.
Stalled, it goes on reckoning.
By small degrees no

one of which could be the smallest,
it's in the same stroke

answering and called to one

small side only, nearer
bit by bit.
Behind it and ahead are both the same.
When with hosts of

more near bits together in their own good time
they make room
upward through the ice and flute it and a great projecting

part of the ice breaks off, to any

one of them, as to any
ice bit too, it's all

one and the same.
Bits are the same continuing
relations and affections.
They are the same as the

same one.

From the littoral
inland at Cape Hold with Hope,

each bit spans as time
itself does on its way to the sun's
going out forever,

each whiles away entrained as

air, ice, rock or water, the belt of land
tall, for the most part, troughed,
drift-mantled,
its tables, deltas and moraines

legato with the syn- and anticline, the banded flaring
promontory walls.